The New Global Society

Globalization
and Development

The New Gl⬤bal Society

Globalization and Development

Eugene D. Jaffe, B.S. (Economics), MBA, Ph.D.
Graduate School of Business Administration
Bar-Ilan University, Israel
Visiting Professor, Copenhagen Business School, Denmark

Foreword by
James Bacchus
Chairman, Global Trade Practice Group
of Greenberg Traurig, Professional Association

Introduction by
Ilan Alon, Ph.D.
Crummer Graduate School of Business
Rollins College

CHELSEA HOUSE
PUBLISHERS
A Haights Cross Communications Company ®
Philadelphia

Cover: Cargo ship docked at a container terminal in Hong Kong.

CHELSEA HOUSE PUBLISHERS

VP, NEW PRODUCT DEVELOPMENT Sally Cheney
DIRECTOR OF PRODUCTION Kim Shinners
CREATIVE MANAGER Takeshi Takahashi
MANUFACTURING MANAGER Diann Grasse

Staff for GLOBALIZATION AND DEVELOPMENT

EXECUTIVE EDITOR Lee Marcott
EDITORIAL ASSISTANT Carla Greenberg
PRODUCTION EDITOR Noelle Nardone
PHOTO EDITOR Sarah Bloom
SERIES AND COVER DESIGNER Keith Trego
LAYOUT 21st Century Publishing and Communications, Inc.

A Haights Cross Communications ✦ Company ®

www.chelseahouse.com

First Printing

9 8 7 6 5 4 3 2 1

Library of Congress Cataloging-in-Publication Data

Jaffe, Eugene D.
    Globalization and development/Eugene D. Jaffe.
       p. cm.—(New global society)
    Includes bibliographical references and index.
    ISBN 0-7910-8186-9 (hard cover)
1. Globalization. 2. Economic development. I. Title. II. Series.
JZ1318.J337 2005
337—dc22

                                                      2005007515

Contents

Foreword

by James Bacchus

IT'S A SMALL WORLD AFTER ALL

One reason that I know this is true is because I have a daughter who adores Walt Disney World in my hometown of Orlando, Florida. When Jamey was small, she and I would go to Walt Disney World together. We would stand together in a long line waiting to ride her very favorite ride—"Small World." We would stand together in those long lines over and over again.

Jamey is in high school now, but, of course, she still adores Walt Disney World, and she and I still stand together from time to time in those same long lines—because she never tires of seeing "Small World." She is not alone. Seemingly endless lines of children have stood waiting for that same ride through the years, hand in hand with their parents, waiting for the chance to take the winding boat ride through Disney's "Small World." When their chance has come, they have seen the vast variety of the world in which we live unfold along the winding way as it appears to the child in all of us. Hundreds of dancing dolls adorn an array of diverse and exotic settings from around the world. In the echoing voice of a song they sing together—over and over again—they remind all those along for the ride that ours is a world of laughter, a world of tears, a world of hopes, and a world of fears.

And so it is. So it appears when we are children, and so it surely appears when we put childhood behind us and try to assume our new roles as "grown-ups" in what is supposed to be the adult world. The laughter, the tears, the hopes, the fears, are all still there in a world that, to our grown-up eyes, keeps getting smaller every day. And, even when we are no longer children, even when we are now grown-ups, we don't really know what to do about it.

The grown-up name for our small world is "globalization." Our globalizing world is getting smaller every day. Economically and otherwise, our world is becoming a place where we all seem to be taking the same ride. Advances in information, transportation, and many other technologies are making distance disappear, and are making next-door neighbors of all of us, whatever our nationality, whatever our costume, whatever the song we sing.

When Walt Disney first introduced the "Small World" ride at the World's Fair in New York in 1964, I was in high school, and we could still pretend that, although the world was getting smaller, it still consisted of many different places. But no more. The other day, I took a handheld device, called a "BlackBerry," out of my pocket and e-mailed instructions to a colleague in my law firm regarding a pending legal matter. I was on a train in the Bavarian mountains in Germany, while my colleague was thousands of miles away in the United States. In effect, we were in the same small place.

This is just one example of our ever-smaller world. And, however small it seems to me in my middle age, and however smaller it may become in my lifetime, it is likely to shrink all the more for my daughter Jamey and for every other young American attending high school today.

Hence, we announce this new series of books for high school students on some of the results of globalization. These results inspire hope, shown in the efforts of so many around the world to respond to the challenges posed by globalization by making international laws, building international institutions, and seeking new ways to live and work together in our smaller world. Those results also inspire fear, as evidenced by streets filled with anti-globalization protesters in Seattle, London, and other globalized cities around the world.

It is hard to tell truth from fiction in assessing the results of globalization. The six volumes in this series help us to do so. Does globalization promote worldwide economic development, or does it hinder it? Does it reduce poverty, or does it increase it? Does it enhance culture, or does it harm it? Does it advance the cause of human rights, or does it impede it? Does it serve the cause of workers' rights, or does it slow it? Does it help the environment, or does it hurt it? These are the important questions posed in these volumes. The hope is that in asking these questions the series will help young people find answers to them that will prove to be better than those found thus far by "grown-ups."

I have had the privilege of trying to begin the process of finding some of these answers. I have helped negotiate international trade agreements for the United States. I have served as a member of the Congress of the United States. I have been one of seven jurists worldwide on the court of final appeal that helps the 148 countries that are Members of the World Trade Organization to uphold international trade rules and to peacefully resolve international trade disputes. I am one of these who see far more reason for hope than for fear in the process of globalization.

I believe we will all be more likely to see globalization in this way if we recall the faces of the dancing dolls in Disney's "Small World." Those dolls are from many different countries. They wear many different costumes. But their faces are very much the same. The song they sing is the same. And, in that song, they remind us all that as we all ride together, "There's so much that we share, that it's time we're aware it's a small world, after all." Indeed it is. And, if we remember all that we in the world share—if we remember above all, our shared humanity—then we will be much more likely to make globalization a reason to hope that our smaller world will also be a better world.

James Bacchus
Chairman, Global Trade Practice Group
of Greenberg Traurig, Professional Association
April 2005

Introduction
by Ilan Alon

Globalization is now an omnipresent phenomenon in society, economics, and politics, affecting industry and government, and all other walks of life in one form or another. THE NEW GLOBAL SOCIETY series gives the reader a well-rounded understanding of the forces of globalization and its multifaceted impact on our world. The international flavor is evident in the make-up of the authors in the series, who include one Israeli, one New Zealander, one Bulgarian, one Korean, and two American scholars. In addition to an international slate of authors, many of whom have lived and worked around the world, the writers hail from fields as diverse as economics, business, comparative literature, and journalism. Their varied experiences and points of view bring a comprehensive and diverse analysis to the topics they write about.

While the books were written to stand alone, those readers who complete all six will find many points of commonality between the books and many instances where observations from one book can be directly applied to points made in another.

These books are written for the lay person and include definitions of key terms and ideas and many examples that help the reader make the ideas more concrete. The books are short and non-technical and are intended to spur the reader to read more about globalization outside these books and in other sources such as magazines, newspapers, journals, Internet sources, and other books on the topics. The discussion of the positive and negative aspects of the consequences of globalization, both here and abroad, will allow the reader to make their own judgments about the merits and demerits of globalization.

A brief description of each of the six books in the series follows:

Globalization and Development—Eugene D. Jaffe
Eugene D. Jaffe of the Graduate School of Business, Bar-Ilan University, Israel, and current Visiting Professor at Copenhagen Business School, Denmark, explains the key terms and concepts of globalization and its historical development. Specifically, it ties globalization to economic development and examines globalization's impact on both developed and developing countries. Arguments for and against globalization are presented. The relevance of globalization for the American economy is specifically addressed.

There are many illustrations of the concepts through stories and case examples, photographs, tables, and diagrams. After reading this book, students should have a good understanding of the positive and negative aspects of globalization and will be better able to understand the issues as they appear in the press and other media.

Globalization and Labor—Peter Enderwick
Peter Enderwick is Professor of International Business, Auckland University of Technology, New Zealand, and a long-time researcher on international labor issues. His book provides a discussion of the impact of globalization on labor with a focus on employment, earnings, staffing strategies, and human resource management within global business. Contemporary issues and concerns such as offshore sourcing, labor standards, decreasing social mobility, and income inequality are treated. The book contains many case examples and vignettes illustrating that while globalization creates

both winners and losers, there are opportunities to increase the beneficial effects through appropriate policy.

Globalization and Poverty—Nadia Ballard

Nadia Ballard is a professional international business consultant with clients in the United States and Europe and is an adjunct instructor for international business at Rollins College, Winter Park, Florida. In addition to her extensive experience living and working in various countries, Nadia is also a native of Bulgaria, a developing country that is struggling with many of the issues discussed in her book.

Globalization, which is reshaping our society at all levels from the individual to the national and regional, is also changing the way we define poverty and attempt to combat it. The book includes the ideas of academics and researchers as well as those who are charged at the practical level with grappling with the issues of world poverty. Unlike other books on the subject, her aim is not to promote a certain view or theory, but to provide a realistic overview of the current situation and the strategies intended to improve it. The book is rich with such visual aids as maps, photographs, tables, and charts.

Globalization and the Environment—Ho-Won Jeong

Howon Jeong teaches at the Institute for Conflict Analysis and Resolution at George Mason University and is author of *Global Environmental Policymaking*. His new book for Chelsea House discusses the major global impacts of human activities on the environment including global warming, ozone depletion, the loss of biological diversity, deforestation, and soil erosion, among other topics. This book explores the interrelationship of human life and nature. The earth has finite resources and our every action has consequences for the future. The effects of human consumption and pollution are felt in every corner of the globe. How we choose to live will affect generations to come. The book should generate an awareness of the ongoing degradation of our environment and it is hoped that this awareness will serve as a catalyst for action needed to be undertaken for and by future generations.

Globalization, Culture, and Language—Richard E. Lee

Richard E. Lee teaches comparative literature at the College of Oneonta, State University of New York. The author believes that globalization is a complex phenomenon of contemporary life, but one with deep ties to the past movements of people and ideas around the world. By placing globalization within this historical context, the author casts the reader as part of those long-term cultural trends.

The author recognizes that his American audience is largely composed of people who speak one language. He introduces such readers to the issues related to a multilingual, global phenomenon. Readers will also learn from the book that the cultural impacts of globalization are not merely a one-way street from the United States to the rest of the world. The interconnectedness of the modern world means that the movements of ideas and people affect everyone.

Globalization and Human Rights—Alma Kadragic

Alma Kadragic is a journalist, a writer, and an adjunct professor at Phoenix University. She was a writer and producer for ABC News in New York, Washington D.C., and London for 16 years. From 1983–89 she was ABC News bureau chief in Warsaw, Poland, and led news coverage of the events that led to the fall of Communism in Poland, Hungary, Czechoslovakia, East Germany, and Yugoslavia.

Her book links two of the fundamental issues of our time: globalization and human rights. Human rights are the foundation on which the United States was established in the late

18th century. Today, guarantees of basic human rights are included in the constitutions of most countries.

The author examines the challenges and opportunities globalization presents for the development of human rights in many countries. Globalization often brings changes to the way people live. Sometimes these changes expand human rights, but sometimes they threaten them. Both the positive and negative impacts of globalization on personal freedom and other measures of human rights are examined. She also considers how the globalization of the mass media can work to protect the human rights of individuals in any country.

All of the books in THE NEW GLOBAL SOCIETY series examine both the pros and the cons of the consequences of globalization in an objective manner. Taken together they provide the readers with a concise and readable introduction to one of the most pervasive and fascinating phenomena of our time.

Dr. Ilan Alon, Ph.D
Crummer Graduate School of Business
Rollins College
April 2005

What is Globalization?

Globalization, as defined by rich people like us, is a very nice thing . . . . You are talking about the Internet, you are talking about cell phones, you are talking about computers. This doesn't affect two-thirds of the people of the world.

—President Jimmy Carter

Small and Smaller*

Jerry Rao wants to do your taxes. Ah, you say, you've never heard of accountant Jerry Rao, but the name sounds vaguely Indian. Anyway, you already have an accountant. Well, Jerry is Indian. He lives in Bangalore. And, you may not know it, but he may already be your accountant.

"We have tied up with several small medium and medium-size C.P.A. firms in America," explained Mr. Rao, whose company, MphasiS, has a team of Indian accountants able to do out-sourced accounting work from across the United States. All the necessary tax data is scanned by U.S. firms into a database

1

that can be viewed from India. Then an Indian accountant, trained in U.S. tax practices, fills in all the basics.

"This is happening as we speak—we are doing several thousand returns," said Mr. Rao. American C.P.A.s don't even need to be in their offices. They can be on a beach, said Mr. Rao, "and say, 'Jerry, you are particularly good at doing New York returns, so do Tom's returns' ... " He adds, "We have taken the grunt work" so U.S. accountants can focus on customer service and thinking creatively about client needs.

Source: Thomas L. Friedman, "Small and Smaller," Copyright © 2004 The New York Times Co. Reprinted with permission.

The word "globalization" has become a buzzword that some use to describe almost everything that is happening in the world today. Some examples that might be termed evidence of globalization include:

- Sending a multinational group of astronauts on a mission to the moon

- The failure of a Swiss bank that has branches in the United States and some European countries

- The establishment of a trade agreement between the United States, Canada, and Mexico

- The visit of a Russian circus troupe to Belgium, France, and Italy

- The ability of a television viewer in the United States to watch a live show broadcast from a foreign TV station.

Design of new computer chips can be done in Silicon Valley and produced in East Asia. Software programs for American companies can be contracted out to firms in India or Ireland and e-mailed back to the United States.

As we enter a world where the price of digitizing information—converting it into little packets of ones and zeros and then transmitting it over high-speed data networks—is dropping to near zero, it means the so-called global village, with quick access to information anywhere in the world, is really here. It means that many jobs people can now do from an office in this country—whether data processing, reading an X-ray, basic accounting, or data processing—can now also be done from someone's office in India or China. Doctors in one country can diagnose patients in another country using MRI images and other data. What do all of these examples have in common? They occur across national boundaries and thus include or affect people in many countries. The verb globalize is defined in the Merriam-Webster dictionary as "to make worldwide in scope and application." This would encompass phenomena that do not simply occur only in one country, but affect a wide range of people on a regional or global basis. Let's look at some more examples.

A couple of decades ago, the NBA basketball league in the United States was composed of teams that were entirely made up of American players. Moreover, basketball was considered to be primarily an American sport. Little by little, basketball became popular around the world, especially in Western European countries. Today there are some star players worldwide that rival the best talent in the United States. The sport has been globalized; it is popular in South America, Asia, and Eastern Europe. Those same countries have flooded the NBA with players who are talented enough to make the rosters at the All-Star Game. Overall, there were 67 international players from 33 countries on NBA rosters in 2004. The NBA All-Star Game looks like a scene from the United Nations. In 2004, the game was televised live to 212 countries in 42 languages, reaching a global audience of nearly 3.1 billion viewers. In addition, there were over 300 media representatives covering the game from 41 countries.

A similar trend has occurred in Europe. Almost every national European sports team is composed of players from different countries, including many from the United States. We thus have something akin to a two-way flow of players; from the rest of the world to United States teams, and from United States teams to the rest of the world. The next step in this process would be the formation of a world basketball league, where North America, Europe, Asia, and other regions would host teams that would compete with each other. In addition to the National Basketball League (or in place of it!), we would have a Global Basketball League.

Let's take another example. You are watching the opening of the Olympic Games in Athens, Greece, that is simultaneously broadcast all over the world via satellite technology that was developed in France and manufactured in the United States, Great Britain, and Ireland. You see an assemblage of athletes from over 100 countries that will compete in a variety of sports that are played in each country. While watching the games, you are eating crackers imported from Italy and drinking bottled water from France. Some of the clothing you are wearing was made in Sri Lanka. Your Nike athletic shoes were made in Malaysia by Chinese ethnic workers. Your Japanese-branded Sony TV set was assembled in Taiwan. Globalization has entered your living room!

With these examples in mind, let us consider a more formal definition of **globalization** as the trend towards a single, integrated, and interdependent world. Globalization can also be considered as the breaking down of traditional barriers between countries that allows the movement of goods, capital, people, and information. This process has speeded up dramatically as technological advances make it easier for people to travel, communicate, and do business internationally. In other words, the world is slowly becoming borderless.

Borderless

Board a train in Malmo, Sweden's third-largest city, and
in under half an hour you are whisked above the waves to
Denmark's capital, Copenhagen. The Oresund rail-and-
car bridge was at last opened three years ago [in 2000],
after a century of talks, nine years of construction and an
outlay of Skr [the Swedish unit of currency, the Krona]
15 billion ($1.9 billion).

The Swedes and the Danes were not always the best
of friends—Denmark ruled this part of Sweden until
1658—but these days the two countries are good EU
[European Union] neighbors. They want their respective
citizens to be able to cross the shared border more easily,
as well as to encourage foreign investors to use the area
as a hub of development for the Nordic and Baltic
regions. The new bridge puts Copenhagen international
airport as close to Malmo as it is to the Danish capital
(a mere 15 minutes either way).

The newly named Oresund region of 3.5 million people
is now developing ties that would not have been possible
without the bridge, such as a network of 12 Danish and
Swedish universities with 140,000 students and 100,000
researchers, and a "medicon" valley with food, medical,
and biotech companies that already employ 26,000 people.

Is the Denmark-Sweden case in the box "Borderless" typical
of what is happening in the world today? Open borders have
made possible a booming tourist industry. In 1959, there were
25 million international tourist arrivals. By 2002, this figure had
increased by over 27 times to about 650 million.[1] Liberalization
of immigration policies around the world has increased the

number of immigrants. Populations of developed countries are becoming globalized, owing to the large numbers of immigrants admitted every year. Among developed countries, Australia and Canada have the highest percentage of foreign-born to the total population, 24 and 19 percent, respectively. The United States comes next, with 11 percent, followed by France and Germany with 9 percent each. Most other developed countries have lower ratios of foreign-born to the total population. However, what is significant is the fact that since 1990, there has been an increase in these ratios for most developed countries. This means that borders are being more open not just for tourists, but also for immigrants.[2]

Not the ratios but also the source of immigrants differ from country to country. In the case of Australia in recent years, a high proportion of immigrants originated from New Zealand, the United Kingdom and China, in that order. China, India, Pakistan, and the Philippines were the source of Canadian immigration, while Mexico has been the main source of immigrants to the United States (about 20 percent of the total), but there have been sizeable contingents from the Philippines and China as well.[3]

Advances in technology have made it easier and less costly for people to communicate with each other. One such technological breakthrough was the facsimile, or fax, machine. While this may appear to be a recent discovery, the first facsimile equipment for use in communications was the chemical telegraph invented by Alexander Bain (1810–1877) in 1842 and patented during the following year. The equipment consisted of a metallic contact resting on a moving paper slip saturated with an electrolytic solution. The solution enabled the conducting of electricity. The wire and the tape formed part of an electric circuit, and when current flowed, discoloration of the tape occurred.

It is thought that the first working model of Bain's chemical telegraph was constructed and operated at about the time of the World's Fair held in London in 1851. At the Fair, a second facsimile machine was demonstrated. The need to have material photographed to provide a negative for transmission, and the consequential high cost of the equipment needed, led to further research and the evolution of a system of transmission based on reflected light. In 1935, the Associated Press news network installed a countrywide network based on this system. Although suitable telephone coupling devices were available from the 1930s, it was not until the 1960s that relatively cheap facsimile machines were available. Growth in the market was prompted by declining postal services in the United States, and in Japan by the pictorial nature of the alphabet. These new machines became known as document facsimile machines and were used for transmitting handwritten, typed, or printed text and drawings. Until the 1980s, facsimile machines were not widely used for global communication, mainly because of the lack of an international standard for their use. Once a standard was agreed upon, facsimile machines became used widely for communication between countries.

Today, global communication is aided by computers, the Internet, mobile phones, and other devices. People, businesses, and governments are linked in a virtual communication network. This linkage will be discussed in the chapters that follow.

Conceptions
and Participants

*Microchips, satellites, fiber optics, and the Internet . . . are able
to weave the world together. . . . [They] allow companies to locate
different parts of their production, research, and marketing in
different countries, but tie them together through computers and
teleconferences as though they were in one place.*

—Thomas L. Friedman,
The Lexus and the Olive Tree: Understanding Globalization

In the previous chapter, we defined globalization as a process that removes barriers to the movement of people, goods and services, and information. In this chapter, we will discuss these barriers and the extent to which they have disappeared. We will also examine the concept of globalization: What does it mean and who are the participants?

MOVEMENTS OF GOODS, CAPITAL, AND PEOPLE

Prior to World War II, governments attempted to protect domestic industry by levying high taxes against the importation of goods from other countries. High taxes made many imported goods relatively expensive compared to domestically produced goods. Thus, domestic manufacturers were protected against foreign competition. Some domestic manufacturers took advantage of this protection and increased the prices they charged their customers. Trade wars sometimes erupted as governments attempted to provide more protection for domestic industry by levying even more taxes on imports or by restricting the quantity of goods that could be imported. Eventually, countries came to the conclusion that most would be better off if competition among them would increase. This could only be accomplished through trade liberalization.

Following the war, a number of international organizations were formed in order to liberalize trade among nations. The first of these was the **General Agreement on Tariffs and Trade (GATT)**, which was established in 1947 by 24 countries. The major objectives of the GATT were the reduction in existing **tariffs** (a percentage or absolute tax on the value of imports) and other trade restrictions, and the settlement of trade disputes. Since the GATT's establishment, tariffs have been reduced through a series of giant bargaining sessions. Whenever a member nation agreed to reduce a tariff rate on any product, the reduction in that product was made available to all members of the GATT. The result of these negotiations was a reduction in the world's tariff levels to about one-fourth of what they had been at the end of World War II.

In 1995, the GATT was succeeded by the **World Trade Organization (WTO)**, which is now the only global international organization that deals with the rules of trade between nations. It was negotiated and signed by most of the world's trading nations and ratified by their governments (Table 2.1). The goal of the WTO is to help producers of goods and services, exporters, and importers conduct their business with a minimum of red tape.

Another significant international organization that was established following World War II was the European Economic Community (EEC), created by the Treaty of Rome, signed in March 1957 by France, Germany, Italy, Belgium, Holland, and Luxembourg. In 1972, Great Britain, Ireland, and Denmark were added, and by the mid-1980s, Greece, Portugal, and Spain

Table 2.1   Some Facts About the World Trade Organization

Location: Geneva, Switzerland
Established: January 1, 1995
Created by: Uruguay Round negotiations (1986–94)
Membership: 146 countries (as of April 4, 2003)
Budget: 154 million Swiss francs for 2003
Secretariat staff: 550
Head: Supachai Panitchpakdi (director-general)
Functions:
- Administering WTO trade agreements
- Forum for trade negotiations
- Handling trade disputes
- Monitoring national trade policies
- Technical assistance and training for developing countries
- Cooperation with other international organizations

became EEC members. Today, the organization, now called the **European Union (EU)**, has 25 members, including Eastern European countries such as Poland and Hungary.

The EU represents by far the largest of the world's regional trading arrangements, and the combined population of its member countries numbers some 500 million. Its objectives are the elimination of all restrictions on the movement of goods and services, capital, and people among its members. An overall goal is to reach full economic union, meaning in part, one currency (the **euro €**), and one monetary system (one central bank, similar to this country's Federal Reserve System) throughout the EU countries.

In most developed countries, the movement of capital has been liberalized. Suppose you have a bank account in New York. You can transfer your money freely to a relative in London, England, by simply making a phone call to your bank branch. If you want to make a purchase from a German company advertised on the Internet, you may do so using a credit card. Large companies transfer capital from one country to another in the same manner. For example, the Ford Motor Company has subsidiaries and dealers located throughout the world. It produces not only the well-known American brands such as Lincoln and Mercury, but also foreign brands such as Aston Martin and Jaguar (UK), Volvo (Sweden), and Mazda (Japan). If company headquarters located in Dearborn, Michigan, decides to build a new plant in the United Kingdom(UK), funds for this purpose may originate from its operations in the United States or from its operations in other countries. Moreover, part of the profits from overseas operations may be transferred to the United States. All of these capital movements may be unrestricted, although they may be subject to tax laws in the various countries.

All of the transactions described above are paid by exchanging one currency for another, except in most countries of the European Union that have one common currency, the euro. If you purchase a book from a store in London via the Internet, your credit card account will be charged the book's price equivalent in dollars, but your bank will pay the store in British pounds. This is called a foreign exchange transaction, the exchange of one currency for another. Staggering amounts of money are shifted around the world every day at the click of a button on someone's computer. These foreign exchange transactions now amount to $1.2 trillion per day!

Mobility of people generally refers to the ability to migrate from one country to another. Generally speaking, migration is motivated by the desire to improve one's economic status and/or degree of freedom. Thus, migration trends generally have been from developing to developed countries and from politically unstable regions to stable ones. Some countries have large migrant populations. About 74 percent of the United Arab Emirates' population and 59 percent of Kuwait's population consists of migrants. Some Western countries also have high migrant populations. Examples include Switzerland and Australia (25 percent), New Zealand (23 percent), and Canada (19 percent).

Most countries still limit the number and source of immigrants, although some give consideration to political refugees fleeing persecution in their home countries. One of the most liberalized areas in the world is the European Union. Citizens of the EU can work in any of the member countries, subject to fulfilling specific work standards such as those required of physicians and lawyers.

While the enlargement of the EU from 15 to 25 countries on May 1, 2004, was accompanied by ceremonies and a lot of goodwill, the original 15 can apply immigration quotas on citizens of the 10 joining countries for a period of up to 7 years. Germany, Italy, and Sweden announced that they would apply this rule in full, while others, such as the UK, Greece, and Belgium, will apply the rule partially.

THE MOVEMENT OF INFORMATION

The movement of information from one country to another occurs by television and radio stations, the Internet, telephone, fax, and other means. The telecommunications industry has historically been heavily regulated by governments. Among the areas regulated include market entry and access to networks. It is beyond the scope of this book to cover all of these aspects. However, one field that is familiar to most is the area of mobile phones, and it provides an excellent example of globalization. The ability to use your mobile phone as you travel from one country to another depends upon the willingness of each government to subscribe to the same broadcasting standard. Yet in the 1980s, even as business was becoming increasingly international, the communications industry focused on exclusively local cellular solutions, none of which was remotely compatible with any of the others. The NMT 450 system operated in the Nordic and Benelux (**Bel**gium, the **Net**herlands, and **Lux**embourg) countries, the TACS system in the UK, C-Netz in West Germany, Radiocom 2000 in France, and RTMI/RTMS in Italy. As you traveled from one country to another, you had to change the band.

This is not the case today. In 1982, the Group Spéciale Mobile, known more popularly as GSM, was established. GSM is a trans-European mobile phone network that includes 500 operators in

207 countries, including the United States. GSM has more than 998 million customers around the world (73 percent of the world's digital mobile market). In addition, there are some 130 key manufacturers and suppliers to the GSM industry. Today, your mobile phone, using GSM technology, switches automatically to a local carrier as you travel from one country to another.

As we have seen, globalization is essentially the emergence of a global marketplace for the production, distribution, and consumption of goods and services and information. It may be described as a three-dimensional concept—it is a *phenomenon*, a *process*, and a *philosophy*. Let's look at the three Ps of globalization more closely.

GLOBALIZATION AS A PHENOMENON

Globalization is a phenomenon that connects people throughout the world. All of us on Earth share the same environment, but many of us were not entirely aware of this until we were told about the dangers of global warming and "mad cow" disease. Globalization is making the world smaller in space and time.

Not only is the world becoming smaller in space and time, but it is also becoming much smaller semantically, according to one writer (see "Get Out of My Namespace"). The world seems to be running out of names, and globalization is partially to blame. Because of instant communication, the spread of business around the world, and the Internet's popularity, it is becoming more difficult to come up with a name that does not belong to someone in cyberspace.

"Get Out of My Namespace"

The German car company known as Dr. Ing. h.c.F. Porsche AG has fought a series of battles to protect the name CARRERA. But another contender is a Swiss village, postal code 7122. "The village Carrera existed prior to the Porsche trademark," Christoph Reuss of Switzerland wrote

to Porsche's lawyers. "Porsche's use of that name constitutes a misappropriation of the good will and reputation
developed by the villagers of Carrera." He added, for good
measure, "The village emits much less noise and pollution
than Porsche Carrera." He didn't mention that José
Carreras, the opera singer, was embroiled in a name
dispute of his own. The car company, meanwhile, also
claims trademark ownership of the numerals 911.

Source: James Gleick, "Get Out of My Namespace," Copyright © 2004
   James Gleick.

GLOBALIZATION AS A PROCESS

Globalization is a process that seeks to eliminate political,
economic, cultural, and geographic distances between peoples.
Participation in international governmental organizations
(IGOs) has been enhanced through organizations like the
North Atlantic Treaty Organization (NATO) and the United
Nations (UN).

   The integration of economies has been accomplished through
increased trade and financial flows and the movement of labor
and knowledge across international borders. Economic groupings like the European Union (EU) seek to eliminate all trade
and investment barriers between them. Many of these countries
have adopted the euro as their official currency, eliminating the
need for individual country currencies. Gone are the French
franc, the German deutschmark, the Spanish peso, the Greek
drachma, and the Dutch guilder, among others. Citizens of these
countries do not need a passport to travel from one country to
another. They also do not need work permits.

   Closer to home is the North American Free Trade Agreement
(NAFTA), a treaty signed between the United States, Canada,
and Mexico that removed tariffs and barriers to trade, services,
and investment between the countries. Similar regional agreements exist between countries of Latin America, Asia, and Africa.

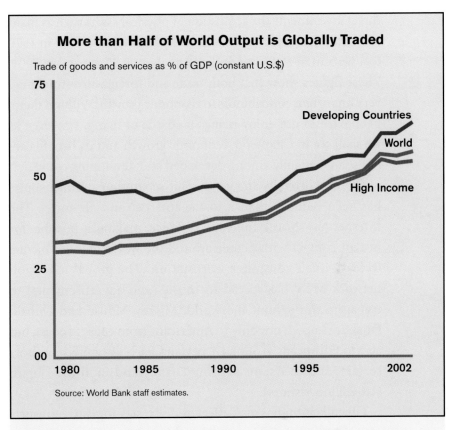

Figure 2.1 In 2002, trade in goods and services as a share of world output reached 54 percent, up from 31 percent in 1980.

These regional economic agreements have been instrumental in the dramatic increase in world trade. The statistics are certainly convincing. Since 1950, the volume of world trade has increased 20 times. From just 1997 to 1999, flows of foreign investment have nearly doubled, from $468 billion to $827 billion. In 2002, trade in goods and services as a share of world output reached 54 percent (Figure 2.1), up from 31 percent in 1980.

The magnitude of trade and foreign investment can also be measured as a percentage of **gross national product**, or **GNP**, the total production of goods and services in an economy. Trade (exports and imports) as a percentage of GNP grew from 28 percent in 1970 to nearly 80 percent in 2001. Likewise, foreign direct investment (the acquistion of physical assets such as plant and equipment) from almost a half percentage of GNP in 1970 to 4 percent in 2000, but declined to about 2.25 percent in 2001. These figures show that both trade and foreign investment are very important contributors to economic growth. Without them, people could not enjoy rising standards of living. However, as we shall see in Chapter 3, economic growth and its benefits are not shared equally among developed and developing countries.

Cultural diversity and geographic separation among peoples has been reduced thanks to the Internet and air travel. The Internet has shrunk time and distance, making it possible for instant contact with people around the world without having to leave one's computer workstation. The global television network MTV has spread its music (and advertisements) to teenagers throughout the world. Mickey Mouse and Donald Duck are known not only to Americans from coast to coast, but also to Europeans visiting Disneyland Paris (12 million visitors so far), and to Asians visiting Disneyland in Tokyo, Japan (18 million visitors).

Globalization has also affected our tastes for different sorts of products and services produced in other countries through travel and tourism and through the migration of peoples. Pizza and pita bread have spread around the world, mainly because of the migration of those who once produced and consumed them in their home country. Centuries ago, wealthy people in Europe first learned about the tea and spices produced in the East as a result of their travel to these areas. As the demand for these products increased, a search was made for ways and means to secure them. America was discovered as a by-product of the search for faster routes of delivery from the Europe to the East!

Globalization has also been affected by public policy and issues of war and peace between nations. Take the case of Port wine, a rich red wine made in Portugal. Its origin was a consequence of hostilities between Britain and France. Traditionally, the British consumed French wines imported from the Bordeaux region. This trade, however, was interrupted during several periods of hostility between the two countries. By the 17th century, the British government began imposing heavy import duties on French wines. Looking for a substitute, the British discovered that Portuguese wines, particularly those from the Douro valley, were to their taste. Traders found that fortifying the red wine with grape brandy both gave the wine an extra alcoholic kick and helped it travel better. The result—a new product called Port wine—remained a favorite in Britain even when the barriers to importing French wines were removed.[4]

GLOBALIZATION AS A PHILOSOPHY

Globalization is also a philosophy that describes the reality of being interconnected. In governments and businesses everywhere, holding a global vision has become the necessary prerequisite for effective policy and strategy. Governments and businesses can no longer make a successful intervention in the political arena or the economy without anticipating and preparing for global consequences. In later chapters of this book, we will discuss the impact of globalization on economic development in greater detail.

WHEN DID GLOBALIZATION BEGIN?

While most agree that globalization is not a recent phenomenon, there is no real consensus about the time when globalization began. Some consider the first milestone of globalization to be the first great expansion of European capitalism in the 16th century, following the first circumnavigation of the earth in 1519 to 1521. Another milestone was the laying of the first successful transatlantic telegraph cable in 1866, which, by providing a real-time communications link between Europe and North America, transformed the information environment. Some argue that globalization took off between 1875 and 1925, which saw the establishment of the International Date Line and world time zones, the near-global adoption of the Gregorian calendar, and the institution of international standards of telegraphy and signaling.

Others believe that globalization began after World War II with the establishment of the United Nations. Globalization was strengthened by the fact that United Nations delegates could decide (but hardly enforce) that how a sovereign government treated its own citizens would no longer be its own business. Towards this end, the Universal Declaration of Human Rights was adopted in 1948 and the ideas of individual choice and dignity began to cross national borders. With the end of the Cold War and the demolition of the Berlin Wall, a new era of globalization occurred. Ideological boundaries collapsed, resulting in the triumph of capitalism over socialism. The United States emerged as the dominant world power.

Others argue that there was just as much globalization in the 19th century as there is today. They cite as proof for their argument that the work force is actually less mobile today than in the 19th century. For example, there was no need for passports, and most people moved freely from one country to another. Sixty million Europeans migrated to North and South America, and Australia. In 1900, 14 percent of the American population was composed of immigrants, compared to some 8 percent today.

In the 1860s and 1870s, many goods were traded freely. For example, 95 percent of German imports were free of duty. According to the "Capital Mobility Index" of the International Monetary Fund, the volume of capital movements in relation to gross national product is less today than in the 1880s. While all of the above may be true, the facts have to be clarified. Trade in the 19th century was primarily in commodities; today it is primarily in goods and services. Capital movements, capital used for acquiring assets abroad, in the 19th century were concentrated in the hands of small groups of wealthy people for long-term investment. Capital movements today are faster, but of shorter term. And while most people today do need passports to enter countries, the volume and scope of travel is much greater than it was during the 19th century.

WHO ARE THE PARTICIPANTS OF GLOBALIZATION?

All of us are influenced in some way by the process of globalization. However, the average person does not have the ability
to influence the process itself. Who are the major players in the
globalization process, those who decide to a large extent what
will be the economic, political, and cultural fortunes of countries, and of course their citizens? Global players may be divided
into three categories: leading actors, or global corporations;
supporting actors, or international governmental organizations
(IGOs); and understudies, or international non-governmental
organizations (NGOs).

Leading Actors: Global Corporations

Global corporations, or **multinational corporations (MNCs)**, are
defined as companies that have their home (or headquarters)
in one country, but have operations and investments in many
others. Examples of such corporations are the major automobile
manufacturers such as Ford, General Motors, and Toyota;
high-tech companies like IBM, Intel, and Motorola; and retail
franchise operations such as McDonald's, Kentucky Fried
Chicken, and Coca-Cola. For example, the McDonald's chain of
restaurants has spread fast-food culture around the world. While
the majority of its outlets are located in developed countries, its
branches in developing countries have increased threefold in the
five years from 1991 to 1996 (Table 2.2).

What distinguishes global corporations from domestic corporations is that the former compete globally, while the latter
compete only in their domestic market. Take the competitors Kodak
and Fuji, for example. Both produce and distribute a wide variety
of products, including film. Both view the world as their market.
Both compete with each other, not only on their home turfs—the
United States and Japan—but also in European markets as well.

Volkswagen is the largest automobile manufacturer in Europe,
but it assembles its cars in plants around the world. While it
sold about 5 million cars in 2003, it sold only 19 percent of its

Table 2.2　McDonald's Restaurants:
Number by Region 1991 & 1996*

REGION	1991	1996
Latin America	212	837
South Asia	0	
South East Asia	113	409
East Asia	123	489
Arab States	0	69
Sub-Saharan Africa	0	17
Developing Countries	448	1,824
Industrial Countries	11,970	19,198
World	12,418	21,022

* Human Development Report, 1998.

cars in its home market, Germany. On the other hand, 36 percent of its cars were sold in Western Europe, 7 percent in Eastern Europe, 16 percent in Asia, 13 percent in North America, and 9 percent in Latin and Central America.[5] Volkswagen is truly a global corporation.

Take the Globalization Quiz*

1. Mitsubishi is a Japanese automobile company.

   Yes ○　　No ○

2. Who wrote the book *The Lexus and the Olive Tree*?

   _____

3. The 1999 anti-globalization protests in Seattle, Washington, were against what international organization?

   _____

4. Which is the most globalized country in the world?

   _____

* Answers are in the back of the chapter.

Supporting Actors: International Governmental Organizations

International governmental organizations (IGOs) are governmental organizations formed by agreements or treaties among nations. There are about 6,500 IGOs in existence today. Some of the most prominent are the International Monetary Fund (IMF); the World Trade Organization (WTO); the United Nations, which not only is active in the political sphere, but also in economic and social endeavors all over the world; banks such as the Asian Development Bank and the European Bank for Reconstruction and Development, which offer loans to developing countries; and political groupings of countries, such as the North Atlantic Treaty Organization (NATO). The International Cocoa Organization is an example of an IGO (Figure 2.2a).

Understudies: Non-Governmental Organizations

Non-governmental organizations (NGOs) are private organizations that pursue activities to protect the environment, provide social services, and undertake economic and community development. These organizations are independent from governments. Since they are not funded by governments, they depend upon charitable donations and voluntary service. They may be found in most countries. NGOs have been classified according to whether they provide relief, such as humanitarian aid, or help in economic development; whether they are religious or secular oriented; or whether they are more active in the private or the public sector. Some NGOs are pro-globalization, while others are anti-globalization. (See Chapter 4 for an in-depth discussion of these terms.) An example of a pro-globalization NGO is the Institute of Public affairs, based in the UK, which is a free-market think-tank that aims to explain free-market ideas, including the benefits of globalization. An example of a generally anti-globalization movement is Public Citizen, an organization founded by Ralph Nader in 1971. While basically devoted to consumer advocacy and accountability in government and

International Cocoa Organization

Figure 2.2a The International Cocoa Foundation's main goal is to foster cooperation between cocoa producers, the industry, and consumers. Its Website home page includes questions and answers about the organization.

business, this organization has focused considerable attention recently on environmental concerns, both in the United States and the world.

It is estimated that there are somewhere between 6,000 and 30,000 NGOs in developing countries alone.[6] Their strength lies in strong grassroots experience and contacts,

Figure 2.2b Greenpeace is a non-governmental organization that works to ensure a peaceful, sustainable environment for future generations. On the home page of its Website it displays some of its current campaigns around the world.

and in an ability to innovate and adapt to difficult circumstances. Their weaknesses include limited financial and management expertise. In spite of these weaknesses, NGOs have managed to channel nearly $10 billion in aid to developing countries. Greenpeace is an example of an NGO (Figure 2.2b).

ANSWERS TO GLOBALIZATION QUIZ

1. No. While the headquarters of Mitsubishi are in Japan, 37 percent of its shares are owned by DaimlerChrysler, which is headquartered in Germany and also has management control.
2. Thomas Friedman
3. World Trade Organization
4. Ireland

What Is the Impact of Globalization?

The popular view that free trade is all very well so long as all nations are free-traders, but that when other nations erect tariffs we must erect tariffs, too, is countered by the argument that it would be just as sensible to drop rocks into our own harbors because other nations have rocky coasts.

—Joan Robinson

In this chapter we discuss how globalization has contributed to the economic development of countries and their residents. The process of globalization in the economic sphere has not always been a smooth one. Not everyone has benefited from globalization, and even among those that have, not all have benefited equally. However, the direction of economic globalization is clear—the economies of nations are becoming more and more integrated.

THE FORCES OF GLOBALIZATION

Three forces have affected the process of economic globalization.[7] First, improvements in technology have reduced the costs of transporting goods, services, and factors of production (such as raw material and components) and of communication. Second, individuals and societies have generally taken advantage of the opportunities provided by the declining costs of communication and transportation. Both of these factors have resulted in increased trade among nations and an increase in tourism. Third, as we discuss next, there has been an increase in the regional economic integration of economies.

REGIONAL ECONOMIC INTEGRATION

Figure 3.1 provides an illustration of what is meant by regional economic integration. The left side of the chart shows a group of nations whose economies are not linked in any way with another nation (a, b, c, d, e, f, g, and h). No individual country is a member of an economic union or group of countries that have signed an agreement to liberalize trade with each other. The right side of the chart shows that most of these countries have formed two clusters or blocs for the purpose of liberalizing trade with each other: G1 (3 countries) and G2 (4 countries). To illustrate this concept, let's assume that countries a, b, and h of the G1 bloc do not charge import taxes on each other's goods. Likewise, the countries c, d, e, and f of the G2 bloc do not charge import taxes on each other's goods. However, country g (in the right-hand chart) has not joined either bloc. If it wants to export its goods to either G1 or G2 countries, its goods will be subject to import taxes. This means that country g may find it difficult to compete in G1 and G2 markets because its goods will be relatively expensive.

What would happen if G1 countries export their goods to G2 countries? The G1 countries' goods would be subject to import taxes because they are not members of the G2 trade agreement. The same would occur if G2 countries would export their goods to G1 countries. Thus, we can expect that trade will increase between the countries in each of these two groups, possibly at the expense of nonmember countries, like g.

Before 1957, there were no regional trade agreements between nations. By 1960, there were two, the European

Regional Economic Integration

Independent Nations

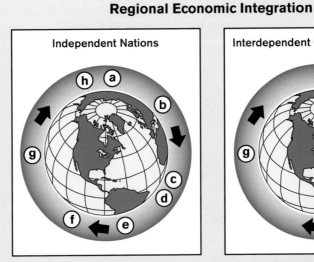

Interdependent Groups of Nations

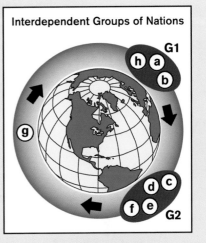

Figure 3.1 This illustration on the left shows a group of nations whose economies are not linked and on the right is shown clusters of nations that have formed blocs to liberalize trade with each other.

Economic Community (EEC) and the European Free Trade Association (EFTA). By 2002, there were 181 agreements, covering every region of the world.[8] We will review the four major regional groupings shown in Table 3.1: the EU, EFTA, the North American Free Trade Agreement (NAFTA), and the Asia-Pacific Economic Cooperation (APEC).

THE EU AND THE EFTA

The European Economic Community (EEC) originally had six founding members: Belgium, France, Germany, Italy, Luxembourg, and the Netherlands. The **European Free Trade Association (EFTA)** countries numbered seven: Austria, Denmark, Norway, Portugal, Sweden, Switzerland, and the United Kingdom. In 1973, Denmark, Ireland, and the United Kingdom joined the EEC, which had now changed its name to the Economic Community (EC). In 1980, Greece became the tenth member, followed by Spain and Portugal in 1986 and

Table 3.1   Comparative Data on Four Major Trade Groups, 2001*

	POPULATION (thousands)	AVERAGE PER-CAPITA GROSS NATIONAL INCOME (U.S.$)
APEC	2,511,000	13,893
EFTA	120,000	18,490
EU	460,493	15,620
NAFTA	405,307	20,490

* Source: World Bank Atlas, 2002.

Austria, Finland, and Sweden in 1995. By now, the organization's name was changed to the **European Union (EU)**, which is its official title today. In 2004, the EU was joined by eight Eastern European countries (the Czech Republic, Estonia, Hungary, Latvia, Lithuania, Poland, Slovakia, and Slovenia) and two Mediterranean countries (Cyprus and Malta). Today, the EU is one of the largest regional economic groups in the world, measured by average per-capita national income.

Since Austria, Denmark, Portugal, Sweden, and the United Kingdom have joined the EU, the EFTA group has been significantly reduced to the membership of only Iceland, Liechtenstein, Norway, and Switzerland. However, this group of four countries still has substantial purchasing power, with an average per-capita national income of $18, 490 (Table 3.1).

The EU is by far the most comprehensive of the world's economic groups. It is the only group that has its own Parliament and one of the only ones to have a judicial court. In addition, most of the 15 countries (before the expansion to 25 in 2004) have adopted a common currency, the euro.

The European Parliament is representative of all member states, proportionate to population size. Parliament members are elected from every member country for a period of five years.

It has responsibility over the EU budget, legislation, and executive decisions made in the areas of foreign affairs, economy and finance, and agriculture.

The European Court of Justice has responsibility over the interpretation and application of EU treaties. A member state, companies, and individuals may appeal to the Court on matters such as competition, freedom of movement of workers, and copyright infringement issues.

With a Parliament, Court of Justice, and single currency, the EU has made the most progress of any regional group of nations towards full economic integration. The four countries of EFTA have abolished tariffs among themselves and permit the free movement of persons, services, and investment. In addition, EFTA members, with the exception of Switzerland, have concluded a free trade agreement with the EU and additional countries, giving it duty-free access to markets with a total population of over 730 million people.

NAFTA–NORTH AMERICAN FREE TRADE AGREEMENT
The **North American Free Trade Agreement (NAFTA)**, which covers the United States, Canada, and Mexico, went into effect in 1994. As shown in Table 3.1, the 3 NAFTA countries have a combined population that is nearly equal in size to that of the 25 EU countries, but have a higher average per-capita national income. Like the EU and EFTA, NAFTA calls for the elimination of most tariffs and non-tariff barriers to trade (measures intended to reduce imports by means other than taxation). Because of the disparity between the economies of Mexico and those of the Canada and the United States, Mexico's tariffs were reduced more slowly. Thus, Mexican industry had more time to adjust to the increased competition that it faces from its more industrialized neighbors.

NAFTA does not go as far as the EU agreement. There are no common governing institutions like the European Parliament or a Court of Justice. The basic standard that underlies NAFTA is national treatment. **National treatment** means that a country treats the activities of its partners the same as it treats domestic activities. For example, foreign goods, services, and investments must be treated the same as domestic goods, services, and investments, once they have cleared customs and have become a part of the country's internal market. National treatment allows each member country to apply its own laws within its own borders. For example, while EU countries must charge the same rate of sales tax on retail sales, NAFTA countries can decide for themselves what sales tax to impose on retail sales (in the United States, because there is no uniform sales tax, this is left up to each state to decide).

APEC–ASIA-PACIFIC ECONOMIC COOPERATION

Asia-Pacific Economic Cooperation (APEC) was founded in 1989 and as of 2004 has 21 members concentrated in Asia and the Pacific Rim (including Australia, New Zealand, China, Singapore, South Korea, the Philippines, and Japan) and in the United States, Canada, Mexico, Peru, and Russia.

Unlike the EU, EEC, and NAFTA, the APEC does not require its members to enter into legally binding obligations, but rather makes decisions by consensus. APEC member countries take individual and collective actions to reduce trade barriers and open their markets. By progressively reducing tariffs and other trade barriers, exports have increased by 113 percent in the first ten years of operation. APEC activities are funded by small annual membership contributions that are used to maintain a Secretariat in Singapore and various projects that support its economic and trade goals.

THE EFFECTS OF ECONOMIC INTEGRATION

There are two main economic effects of integration. First, removal of trade barriers means that it should be more worthwhile for members to trade with each other than with non-members. For example, assume that French companies are importing the same product from Germany and Australia. Both France and Germany are members of the EU and therefore the product imported from Germany is not taxed. Since Australia is not a member of the EU, the product imported from Australia will likely be taxed and therefore be more expensive. The end result is that it will be more profitable for French companies to purchase the product from Germany (which also incurs lower shipping costs). Thus, as a result of integration, imports will be shifted from non-member to member countries. This shift is called **trade diversion**.

A second effect of economic integration occurs when the size of a market grows as import barriers are removed. Barriers to imports protect inefficient (high-cost) producers. When the barriers are removed, and lower-cost imports enter the market, these producers are no longer able to compete at the same price. They either become more efficient, for example, by improving production techniques, or they exit the market. In the case of the French companies above, if trade barriers are removed not only will French companies buy products from Germany, but the French market for German products will also grow because some inefficient French producers will exit the market. This effect is called **trade creation**.

Table 3.2 provides an example of trade creation and trade diversion. Suppose that Australian apples cost 50 cents each. French apples cost 60 cents, and German apples cost 70 cents (Table 3.2, column 1). If there are no national tariffs, Australia is the most efficient apple producer. Australia will produce and export apples to France and Germany. Suppose Germany levies a 15-cent tariff on all apple imports in order to protect its domestic industry (Table 3.2, column 2). Then Australian apples in Germany cost 50 + 15 = 65 cents, and French apples in Germany cost 60 + 15 = 75 cents. Since German apples cost 70 cents, German consumers continue to import Australian apples at a price of 65 cents. The tariff has reduced, but not eliminated, trade between Germany and Australia. Germany no longer imports French apples.

Table 3.2   Price of Apples

	WITHOUT TARIFFS	WITH A 15% GERMAN TARIFF	WITH A TRADING BLOC BETWEEN GERMANY AND AUSTRALIA	WITH A TRADING BLOC BETWEEN FRANCE AND GERMANY
Australian	50*	65*	50*	65
French	60	75	75	60*
German	70	70	70	70

* Lowest Price.

If Germany and Australia form a trading bloc and remove tariffs between them (Table 3.2, column 3), then Australian apples now cost 50 cents in Germany (since there is no tariff) while the price of French apples remains at 75 cents (since French producers must still pay the German tariff). Trade creation has occurred, since the trading bloc generates trade with a more efficient producer. Trade creation increases the welfare of the countries involved (in this case, among the trading bloc countries). Everyone is better off because they can buy apples at a lower price.

If France and Germany form a trading bloc, the tariff on French apples is removed, but not that on Australian apples (Table 3.2, column 4). Thus the price of a French apple in Germany is 60 cents, while the price of an Australian apple is 65 cents. The French apple is artificially cheaper because of the non-neutral treatment of the two countries in terms of the German tariff (0 on France, 15 cents on Australia). Trade is therefore diverted from the lowest cost producer to a more expensive producer due to the trading bloc. Trade diversion may either increase or reduce the welfare of the countries involved. It raises the welfare because, compared to the tariff situation, tariff levels have fallen and trade has expanded. However, it lowers the welfare because trade has been diverted away from the most efficient producers (in this case the Australians).

Note that in both the cases of trade diversion and trade creation, the same effects can occur in all member countries. As a result, the amount of trade between member countries will increase significantly at the expense of non-member countries. And, as trade increases, the economies of member nations grow.

WHAT FORCES PROPEL ECONOMIC INTEGRATION?

Improvements in Transportation

Before the 15th century, the transportation of goods from one continent to another, and even from one country to another, was hazardous, time consuming, and costly. For most goods, shipping by land for more than a few miles was prohibitively expensive.[9] The development of ocean-going sailing vessels in the 15th century was a first stage in the globalization of transportation. However, shipments across oceans were restricted to goods that had high value, such as spices, gold and silver, and silk. Not only was ocean shipping costly, it was also dangerous, subject to the weather and pirates. Over time, shipping vessels became larger and could carry more goods over longer distances, thereby reducing the cost. In spite of this, shipping costs were a significant barrier to trade well into the 1800s.

The invention of steam-powered ships in the second half of the 19th century was another milestone in the globalization of transportation. By the end of the century, the cost of shipping a ton of cargo across the Atlantic was about one-fifth of what it was at the beginning of the century. Average ocean freight and port charges per ton fell from $95 in 1920 to $60 in 1930. In 1990, they were $29, about one-third of what they were in 1920.[10] One of the reasons for the reduction in freight costs was the introduction of containerization. The use of containers to ship goods increased relative to other means over the 20-year period from 1980 to 2000, as shown in Figure 3.2. Containerized cargo increased from about 20 percent of total cargo in 1980 to about 65 percent in 2000.

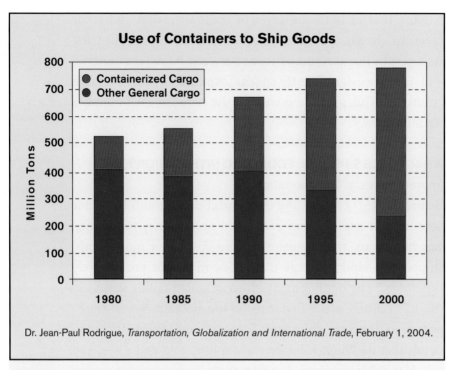

Use of Containers to Ship Goods

● Containerized Cargo
● Other General Cargo

Dr. Jean-Paul Rodrigue, *Transportation, Globalization and International Trade*, February 1, 2004.

Figure 3.2 This graph shows a 20-year period over which the use of containers to ship goods increased relative to other means of moving cargo.

The beginning of commercial air transportation in the 1930s added another milestone to globalization. The cost of air transportation has also decreased substantially over time, from $0.68 per passenger mile in 1930 to $0.11 in 1990.[11]

Improvements in Communication

Both the means and the cost of communication have improved over the last decade. Costs for the main means of communication decreased significantly after World War II, owing to improvements in information technology. For example, a 3-minute phone call from New York to London cost $245 in 1930. The same call cost only $3 in 1990. The Internet has opened up a new world of communication, while also slashing the cost of transactions. For example, making a bank transaction by telephone costs about $.55, making the same transaction in an ATM machine reduces the cost to $.45, by the Internet, to less than $.10. This book, for example, was written for an American publisher, but the author was located in another country. Most of the material on which this book is based was retrieved from university libraries via the Internet without having to set foot in them. Correspondence with the publisher was maintained via e-mail. Thus, this book itself is representative of the globalization process.

Who Are the Talkers?

The use of cell phones is on the rise. Which European countries have the most cell phones per capita? In Austria there are 79 cell phone subscribers per 100 inhabitants. On average, nearly every Austrian has a cell phone. Austria is closely followed by Finland (73 cell phone subscribers per 100 inhabitants), Sweden (71), and Norway (70). The United States has only 40 subscribers per 100 inhabitants. It would seem that people living in less densely populated countries like Finland and Norway have more of a need to connect to one another via the telephone (Norway also has the most telephone lines per 100 inhabitants in Europe).

Some of the same countries are also highly connected to the Internet. Iceland has the highest rate of Internet users per 100 inhabitants in Europe (60), followed by Sweden (56), Norway (49), and the Netherlands (46). In comparison, the United States has 60 Internet users per 100 inhabitants.

WHICH ARE THE MOST GLOBAL COUNTRIES?

Every year, *Foreign Policy* magazine rates countries according to the extent to which they have globalized.[12] Ratings are based on such factors as the number of memberships in international organizations, the use of technology (such as the number of Internet users), the extent of international travel, and economic integration. Table 3.3 shows the top 20 global countries in 2003. Most of the countries are members of the EU, with the exception of Singapore, Canada, the United States, New Zealand, Malaysia, and Israel. Ireland was ranked as the most global, owing to its foreign investment and the development of its high-tech industries. The "three S's"—Switzerland, Sweden, and Singapore—were ranked second, third, and fourth. Further down the ratings was the United States, ranked 11, while Israel and Spain were ranked 19 and 20, respectively.

Measures of Global Development

What country would you like to live and work in? If you live in a developed country like the United States or the UK, you would probably opt to stay where you are. If you live in a less developed country, you might choose a country with a higher standard of living or a higher quality of life. But do the United States and the UK enjoy the highest standard of living and quality of life in the world? Before answering this question, we must define these terms.

As a general rule, a country's development may be measured by changes in a peoples' "standard of living." **Standard of living** is defined as the quality and quantity of goods and services available to people. It is often measured by real income (adjusted for inflation) per person, although other measures may be used, such as ownership of certain goods (number of dishwashers or home computers per 1,000 people), or measures of health, such as life expectancy. However, there are problems in comparing material standards of living between countries. Take, for example, a country that has a small, wealthy upper class and a very large, very poor lower class. The average level of income per person in this country may be relatively high, even though most of the people have a low standard of living. One must therefore be careful in making comparisons between countries.

Table 3.3   Top Global Countries in 2003

1. Ireland
2. Switzerland
3. Sweden
4. Singapore
5. Netherlands
6. Denmark
7. Canada
8. Austria
9. United Kingdom
10. Finland
11. United States
12. France
13. Norway
14. Portugal
15. Czech Republic
16. New Zealand
17. Germany
18. Malaysia
19. Israel
20. Spain

For example, Figure 3.3 shows income per person in the UK from 1970 to 2000, measured in U.S. dollars. There was a significant increase in income from 1996. What caused the increase? A strong British pound since 1996 was mainly responsible for boosting the standard of living in the UK. As noted previously, standard of living may also be measured by ownership of durable goods. Figure 3.4 shows ownership of dishwashers and computers in the UK The chart shows that about 65 percent of the highest income group (10th decile) in the UK have a dishwasher, as opposed to about 5 percent of the lowest income group. Thus, there is a strong relationship between a person's income and his/her ability to purchase durable goods such as dishwashers and computers.

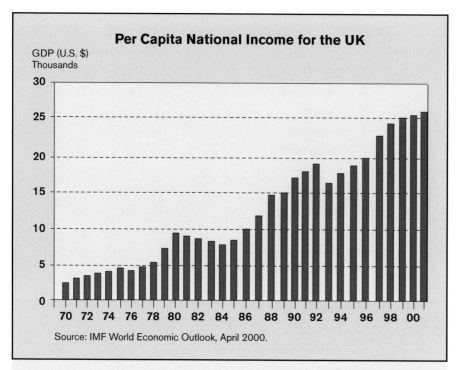

Figure 3.3 This illustration shows the income per person in the UK from 1970 to 1990, measured in U.S. dollars. The strong British pound since 1997 contributed to the betterment of their standard of living.

The standard of living concept may be compared with the term quality of life, which takes into account not only the material standard of living, but also other more subjective factors that contribute to human well-being, such as leisure, safety, cultural resources, social life, social services, and benefits such as unemployment insurance and vacation time. Thus, we have to examine not only material welfare, but also those social welfare factors that contribute to the well-being of a society. So far, we haven't made any comparisons between countries. We still have to answer the question: In which country would you want to live? Objectively, it would be the country that best meets one's basic social and material needs. Which country best fulfills these needs? According to Professor Richard J. Estes, who heads the Program in Social and Economic Development at the School of

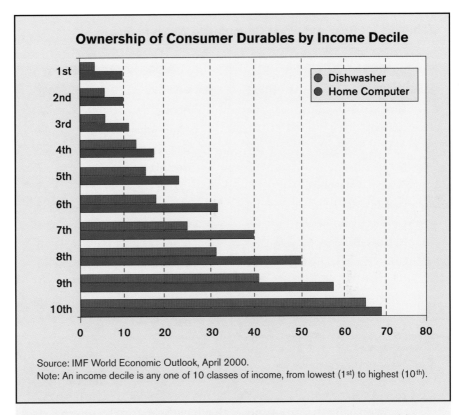

Figure 3.4 The ownership of some big-ticket items, represented by computers and dishwashers, in the UK. There is a strong relationship between a person's income and their ability to buy such items.

Social Work at the University of Pennsylvania, that country is Denmark. Denmark performed best on some 45 social, political, and economic indicators measured by Estes, including health, education, social services, population changes, economic growth, and the impact of military expenditures. However, if you choose not to live in Denmark, what other countries might fit the bill? Table 3.4 shows the best and worst countries to live in according to Professor Estes's measurements.

Basically, the other Scandinavian countries of Finland, Norway, and Sweden are strong contenders for the "best" countries, based on their economic development and social welfare programs. On the bottom of the list, representing the "worst" countries are

Table 3.4   **Best and Worst Countries in Which to Live**

BEST COUNTRIES			WORST COUNTRIES		
RANK	COUNTRY	SCORE	RANK	COUNTRY	SCORE
1	Denmark	98	1	Angola	-25
2	Norway	96	2	Afghanistan	-11
3	Austria, Sweden	93	3	Sierra Leone	-8
4	France	92	4	Somalia	-7
5	Finland, Luxembourg	91	5	Liberia	-5
6	Ireland, Poland	89	6	Mozambique	-3
7	Germany, Italy, Iceland	88	7	Chad, Ethiopia	1
8	Hungary, Slovenia, Belgium	87	8	Niger	5
9	United Kingdom, Portugal	86	9	Eritrea	6
			10	Burkina-Faso, Guinea-Bissau	7
			11	Uganda, Guinea	8
			12	Rwanda	9

Source: 27th Asia and Pacific Regional Conference of the International Council on Social Welfare, Jakarta, Fall, 1997.

Note: The maximum score possible is 100.

primarily African countries that have been torn by internal strife, unemployment, and physical calamities such as drought and flood. These sorts of countries are represented by Angola, Liberia, Mozambique, and Somalia.

Globalization of the Danish Cuisine*

Great changes and increased choices appeared in the Danish cuisine in the 1960s as a result of increased affluence, internationalization, the advent of self-service in the retail trade, the use of electricity in the kitchen, refrigerators and freezers, and also of the increasing number of women going out to work. American influence is obvious with such dishes as salads, pasta, baked potatoes, barbecue, turkey, and ready-to-eat chicken dishes. Italian cuisine has also established itself with for instance pizzas and a widespread use of tomatoes. Meat consumption has risen dramatically, still with pork as the most common kind of meat. The tendency is towards steaks and to minced meat. Gravy and potato dishes still maintain their place, so that sausages and rissoles [croquettes] are the dishes most frequently seen on Danish dinner tables.

---

* Royal Danish Ministry of Foreign Affairs website, "Denmark—Conditions of Life—The Danish Cuisine."

Where was the United States positioned on Professor Estes's list? The United States scored 80 points, which placed it 27th, between Bulgaria and Estonia in the study. This position has deteriorated, since the United States was ranked 18th in 1990. The relatively poor standing of the United States in 1997 was attributed in part to the fact that 37 million Americans were at a poverty level, 40 percent of whom were children under the age of 18. Also cited as an explanation for the country's social decline was the widening income gap between the country's highest and lowest wage earners, the country's deteriorating cities, stagnation in the social progress for women, and growing social tensions.

Shifts in Economic Development

But what about changes in the comparative economic weight of the United States and Western Europe, Japan and the rest of the world? The measure of income as reflected in gross domestic product (GDP) is a good indication of each region's relative economic weight and of economic changes over the 20th century.

On average, over the last 100 years people of all regions of the world improved their standard of living. The average income of Americans and Europeans quadrupled, that of sub-Saharan Africans doubled, and the Japanese improved their standard of living more than any other nation in the world. Figure 3.5 shows the share of the world's GDP in three time periods. Contrary to widely held perceptions of some critics of globalization, the

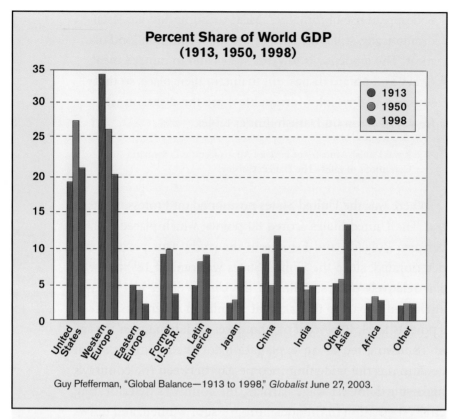

Guy Pfefferman, "Global Balance—1913 to 1998," *Globalist* June 27, 2003.

Figure 3.5 The share of the world's gross domestic product (GDP) is shown here at three time periods. The GDP share of Europe and the United States declined from about 53 percent to about 43 percent from 1913 to 1998. After 1950, Japan increased from 3 to 8 percent. The rest of the world increased its share of world GDP from 45 to 50 percent.

world GDP share of Western Europe and the United States combined declined from about 53 percent to 43 percent from 1913 to 1998. After 1950, Japan increased its share of world GDP from 3 to 8 percent. The rest of the world—which includes developing countries—increased its share of world GDP from 45 to 50 percent.

The economic weight of the United States did not change appreciably during the 20th century. After increasing from 19 percent in 1913 to 27.3 percent in 1950—the U.S. economic weight fell to 22 percent by the end of the 20th century. Western

Europe's share of global GDP declined dramatically—from 34 percent in 1914 to 20 percent in 1998, largely as a reflection of slow population growth. Other Asian countries (including Korea) increased their share of world output—as did China. Latin America increased its share by only 4 percent, reflecting rapid population growth. Between 1913 and 1950, the share of the former Soviet Union and Eastern Europe remained at 13 percent— but fell to just 5 percent combined by 1998.

Global Development under Conditions of Insecurity

One of the most serious constraints to continued economic growth and development is uncertainty caused by political unrest. It is no surprise that those countries that have experienced rapid economic growth have also been the most stable politically. The greatest threat in recent years to economic development has been terrorism. The terrorist attacks in New York on September 11, 2001, and in Madrid on March 11, 2004, have profound economic consequences. In the United States alone, following the September 11th attacks, employers cut more than 248,000 jobs. The transportation system cut 96,000 workers from its payroll.

The economic costs of terrorism have been felt even in those countries that were not immediate targets. These costs have been manifested in reduced consumer confidence and spending, and a downturn in tourism, which has had an especially strong impact on the airline industry. The costs of terrorism are both short and long-term.[13] In the short-run there is the immediate loss of life and property, as occurred on and immediately after September 11. Another immediate effect of terrorism is an increase in apprehension and uncertainty, which is usually evident in financial markets. Over the long run, nations, industries, and individual firms sustain what has become to be known as a "terrorist tax." Increased expenditures for security are necessary at every level of the economy. Security arrangements cause travel delays, longer cross-border inspections for goods, higher insurance costs, intelligence agency upgrades, higher shipping costs, slower mail deliveries, and increased immigration restrictions. More difficult to measure costs include those caused by anxiety and stress associated with the increased uncertainty and threat of terrorism. These costs, which have to be incurred, have a dramatic and negative effect on the quality of life.

Globalization, Good or Bad?

It has been said that arguing against globalization is like arguing against the laws of gravity.

—Kofi Annan, Secretary General of the United Nations

The violent protests that greeted—and disrupted—the World Trade Organization meeting in Seattle in November 1999, and later demonstrations in Prague and Melbourne, reminded us that the process of globalization is controversial. Environmentalist groups, consumer advocates, and human rights activists were among those who have taken to the streets of Seattle and elsewhere to voice their dissatisfaction with the globalization process (Figure 4.1). Why is there dissatisfaction with the outcome of globalization? In this chapter, we examine the anti-globalization movement, and the arguments, both pro and con, over globalization.

THE ANTI-GLOBALIZATION MOVEMENT

Opponents of globalization include groups and organizations with different concerns, cultures, and agendas. They do agree on one thing,

Figure 4.1 Thousands of anti-G8 demonstrators marched peacefully in southeastern France on Sunday, June 1, 2003. (G8 designates eight of the largest industrialized countries in the world.) The anti-globalization movement chose that Sunday as a day of protest against the G8 summit taking place in nearby Evian.

however—that the costs of globalization far outweigh the benefits, and that what benefits there are accrue only to elites and not less advantaged persons. After you have evaluated the information presented in this chapter, you will be able to decide for yourself whether these contentions are correct. However, one thing is clear. There is mixed support for globalization all over the world. The results of the Pew Research Center's Global Attitude surveys taken during 2002 and 2003 among more than 66,000 people in 49 countries showed lukewarm support for globalization in North America and Western Europe (Table 4.1). Surprisingly, the greatest support for globalization came from those in West and East/South Africa, people who are alleged to benefit least from globalization. Young people between the ages of 18–29 and middle-aged people between the ages of 30–49 living in Africa strongly support globalization. In North America and Western Europe, less than half of those polled felt good about the "world becoming more connected through greater economic trade and faster communication." Among those aged 65 and older, only 27 percent in North America and 36 percent in Western Europe felt good about becoming more connected. Older Americans and Western Europeans are more likely than their grandchildren to have doubts about globalization: 43 percent of those aged 18–29 in North America support globalization, while only 27 percent aged 65 and older do so.

The surveys also found that older people tend to worry that their way of life is threatened, to feel that their culture is superior to others, and to support restrictions on immigration. Such a generation gap between expressed opinions is less pronounced in Asia, Africa, and the Middle East. For example, the Pew Center surveys showed that 71 percent of people in the United States aged 65 and older, and 55 percent of those aged 18 to 29 want to be protected from foreign influence. The surveys also showed that the generation gap is greater in Britain, France, and Germany, where older people are twice as likely as young people to be worried about erosion of their way of life. Such feelings seem contrary to the process of globalization, which tends to connect people rather than separate or isolate them. Why then, are many people opposed to globalization? According to Joseph Nye, Professor of International Relations at Harvard University, the concerns of the opponents of anti-globalization fall into three categories: economic, cultural, and political (Table 4.2) [14]

Table 4.1   **Ideas about Globalization**

FOR	AGAINST
Globalization creates employment and income	Globalization leads to income inequality and poverty.
Foreign subsidiaries in developing countries provide investment and employment and pay high wages to workers.	Globalization is being exploited by multinational corporations; globalization exploits workers.
Globalization advances living standards.	Globalization causes financial instability.
Governments voluntarily give up some sovereignty for the gains from trade. Decisions made by organizations like the World Trade Organization are made by consensus.	Government sovereignty is compromised.
Globalization creates jobs.	Globalization exports jobs.
Global companies are working hard to improve their environmental performance.	Global companies place environmentally degrading industries in developing countries.
It is foolish to believe that a world of 6 billion people will somehow form a monoculture.	Globalization will result in the end of cultural diversity.

GLOBAL EQUALITY AND INEQUALITY

The Income and Poverty Gap

The benefits of globalization have not been spread equally among people and countries. It is claimed that the assets of the 200 richest people in the world are greater than the combined income of more than 2 billion people in the poorest countries.[15] It is also generally alleged that the rate of income inequality—the gap between rich and poor—is increasing, in large part because of globalization. For example, the 1999 United Nations Human Development Report states that the income of the

Table 4.2   **Mixed Support for Globalization**

	AGE			
	18–29 %	**30–49** %	**50–64** %	**65+** %
North America	43	35	35	27
Western Europe	41	37	40	36
Eastern Europe	39	30	30	7
Latin America	36	36	44	45
West Africa	75	66	58	61
East/South Africa	59	51	48	31
Conflict Area*	50	50	45	39

Percent responding "very good" to "How do you feel about the world becoming more connected through greater economic trade and faster communication?"

* Countries included in the Middle East/Conflict area are Egypt, Jordan, Lebanon, Pakistan.

richest 20 percent of the world's population was 30 times that of the poorest 20 percent in 1960, but 74 times that of the poorest group in 1977.[16] The same report found that from 1990 to 1999, the number of people earning $1 or less a day remained the same, at 1.2 billion, while the number of people earning less than $2 a day increased from 2.55 to 2.8 billion. This is evidence that the standard of living of a significant proportion of the world's population had not improved over the past decade. Moreover, one-fifth of the world's people living in the highest-income countries had:

- 86 percent of the world's gross national product, while the bottom fifth had only 1 percent.

- 82 percent of the world's exports, while the bottom fifth had only 1 percent.

- 68 percent of foreign direct investment; while the bottom fifth had just 1 percent.

- 74 percent of the world's telephone lines; while the bottom fifth had only 1.5 percent.

Further evidence of a widening income gap between rich and poor countries appeared in the World Economic Outlook published by the International Monetary Fund, an organization that is hardly a foe of globalization.[17] The report concludes that while production per person has increased, the distribution of income between countries has become more unequal than it was at the beginning of the 20th century.

What are the possible links between globalization and poverty? Should rich countries help poor ones? Should international institutions and organizations like the World Bank and the International Monetary Fund assist poor people in developing countries? While it is debatable whether globalization is the sole cause of global inequality, leaders of the developed world have stated that something must be done to reduce poverty and income differentials between have and have-not nations. For instance, at a summit meeting in Okinawa, Japan, on July 23, 2000, the leaders of the **G8** group of industrialized countries (United States, Japan, Great Britain, Germany, France, Russia, Italy, and Canada) issued the following declaration:

> During the last quarter of the 20th century, the world economy has achieved unprecedented levels of prosperity, the Cold War has come to an end, and globalization has led to an emerging common sense of community. Driving these developments has been the global propagation of those basic principles and values consistently advocated by the summiteers— democracy, the market economy, social progress, sustainable development, and respect for human rights. Yet we are keenly aware that even now in many parts of the world, poverty and

injustice undermine human dignity, and conflict brings human suffering.

We must tackle the root causes of conflict and poverty. We must bravely seize the opportunities created by new technologies in such areas as information and communications technology and life sciences. We must acknowledge the concerns associated with globalization, while continuing to be innovative in order to maximize the benefits of globalization for all.[18]

Links between Inequality, Poverty, and Globalization

Globalization requires economies and societies to adapt. Since economies almost never develop equally, some nations will grow faster than others, so that globalization increases inequality. While the growth of income during the 20th century was significant, the gap between rich and poor countries and the gap within countries between the rich and poor have grown. The gross domestic product per capita (or income per person per year) of the richest quarter of the world's population increased nearly fivefold during the 20th century (Figure 4.2), from about $4,000 to nearly $20,000), while the poorest quarter had less than a threefold increase (from less than $1,000 to about $2,800).

The experience of developing countries in catching up to developed countries has also been mixed. Since 1970, incomes in newly industrialized Asian economies, such as Hong Kong, South Korea, Singapore, and Taiwan, have increased significantly towards levels of industrial countries. A large number of developing countries, however, have either remained in place or lost ground. For example, by 1999, Asian countries had reached about 65 percent of the developed countries' GDP per person level. Central and South American countries had reached the 25 percent level (a decline from close to 35 percent in 1971), while African countries had reached only about 10 percent of the level of developed countries (about the same level as in 1971). Additional insight on different rates of growth can be gained from comparing South Korea and Ghana, a country in West Africa. Both countries

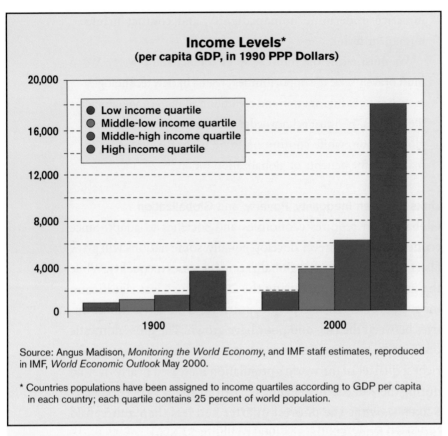

Income Levels*
(per capita GDP, in 1990 PPP Dollars)

● Low income quartile
● Middle-low income quartile
● Middle-high income quartile
● High income quartile

1900   2000

Source: Angus Madison, *Monitoring the World Economy*, and IMF staff estimates, reproduced in IMF, *World Economic Outlook* May 2000.

* Countries populations have been assigned to income quartiles according to GDP per capita in each country; each quartile contains 25 percent of world population.

Figure 4.2 Over the past 100 years the income per person per year of the richest quarter of the world increased fivefold, whereas the poorest quarter had less than a threefold increase. This means that the gap between rich and poor countries has grown.

had the same income per person in 1960. By 2001, however, South Korea had 30 times the per person income as Ghana.

Can globalization be blamed for income disparities like those? Some argue that national government policies, rather than the policies of developed countries or multinational corporations, determine to a large extent whether or not a country's income will grow. Thus, the principal forces for increasing income and for reducing poverty are the national governments themselves, through their decision-making procedures and implementation. According to Marilee S. Grindle, a professor at the Institute for

International Development at Harvard University, more developing countries could benefit from globalization if they had a strong and honest government, rather than a weak and corrupt one.[19] Some claim that the reason why some countries have not advanced economically is that they have isolated themselves from globalization itself. That is, they protect their domestic industries from outside competition by erecting trade barriers.

For globalization to reduce and even erase poverty, its technological forces must reach the more than 2 billion people who live in the developing countries, so they can reap its economic and social benefits. What primarily matters to people in poor countries are the corruption and waste that often undermine their countries' growth prospects. For this to happen, there is an urgent need to reform, redirect, and "humanize" the forces of globalization. According to Jeffrey Sachs, an economist and faculty member of Columbia University, three major things need to happen for globalization and technology to help poor countries. First, the impact of public health and ecology must be brought into the analysis of technological change and economic growth. Second, governments need to change their approach to foreign aid; they should spend more, and more wisely. Third, participation in international assistance needs to be broadened and recast. Thus, multinational firms and first-world universities, like Columbia and Harvard, and scientific establishments should be part of the effort to promote and spread technology, and the official agencies charged with global development, such as the World Bank, the International Monetary Fund, and several United Nations agencies, should be reformed.[20]

Globalization Creates Employment

From time to time, the **International Labour Organization (ILO)**, an agency of the United Nations, requests the governments of developed and developing countries to describe the action taken by their multinational companies to increase

Table 4.3 Activities of Multinational Companies

COUNTRY	ACTION REPORTED BY GOVERNMENTS AND LABOR UNIONS
Bahamas	MNCs have significantly expanded their activities, leading to an increase in the demand for labor. Several thousand new permanent jobs have been created. Working conditions have been improved. MNCs hold consultations prior to starting operations in order to keep their manpower plans in harmony with national social development policies.
Barbados	MNCs expand their activities in different sectors of the economy, thereby increasing employment opportunities. MNCs are granted permission to operate only after they have met all basic requirements as specified by law, or custom and practice.
Brazil	MNCs have made a great contribution by bringing in private investment capital, stimulating industrial development and exports, utilizing local raw material, components and services, and creating jobs. Wages and benefits are among the best in Brazil, even though wages are noticeably lower than those paid in the home country.
Cambodia	In the context of national reconstruction following more than 20 years of war, MNCs contribute to remedying unemployment by recruiting young people. MNCs organize training programs, send their trainees to developed countries for further training, and contribute to the local development of woodwork, more specifically cabinet-making.
Czech Republic	There is no difference in the conduct of MNCs and local employers as regards employment. Acquisitions of local companies by MNCs have been accompanied by staff cuts and organizational changes in order to improve productivity. New investment and growth in output have led to a gradual

employment opportunities and the extent to which these companies cooperate with government actions in combating unemployment. In addition, the ILO formulates international labor standards intended to ensure the basic rights of workers, including the right to organize unions, to collective bar-

increase in employment. The role of MNCs in the labor market is largely positive. They provide a degree of economic stability and frequently locate their operations in areas with relatively low levels of employment.

Sri Lanka	The main benefit of MNCs to workers in Sri Lanka is the creation of employment opportunities. However, most MNCs do not provide favorable terms of employment and working conditions.
Turkey	MNCs contribute to job creation, but there is no precise quantitative or qualitative information in this regard. The acquisition of large local companies by MNCs through privatization could result in a decrease in jobs prior to and after operations. MNCs have acted in accordance with the law and the collective agreement regarding the recruitment and advancement of nationals.
Ireland	MNCs have created direct employment for 100,000 persons and the same number of indirect jobs. Before starting their operations, they hold consultations in order to keep their manpower plans in harmony with national social development policies. Priority is given to the employment, promotion, and advancement of nationals, and these enterprises have contributed to the local development and use of appropriate technologies that have had positive effects on employment.
United States	Between 1988 and 1993 the number of persons working in U.S. affiliates of foreign-owned enterprises rose from 3.8 million to over 4.7 million—5 percent of the work force in the non-banking sector.

gaining, and to equality of opportunity and treatment at the workplace.

Table 4.3 above summarizes some of the actions taken by multinational companies (MNCs) in 9 countries out of a total of 74 developed, developing, and emerging economy countries

Table 4.4	The Four Largest Multinational Corporations Compared to Country Gross Domestic Product* (2002, $Billions)	
Wal-Mart Stores		246.5
Sweden		233.4
Austria		230.7
Greece		227.7
Ukraine		203.3
Malaysia		198.4
Portugal		195.2
General Motors		186.7
Exxon Mobil Corporation		182.5
Royal Dutch/Shell Group		179.4
Algeria		173.8
Romania		169.3
Denmark		155.3
Norway		149.1
Finland		133.8

Source: *Fortune Magazine.*

surveyed. On the whole, the governments and labor unions reported that MNCs made a positive contribution to their economies, resulting in increased employment and worker training. Note, for example, the considerable proportion of workers employed in the subsidiaries of foreign-owned MNCs operating in the United States. These contributions held for both developing and developed countries alike. There were a few exceptions, notably in Sri Lanka, where the acquisition of domestic companies by MNCs reportedly led to staff cuts and the below-expected working conditions.

GLOBALIZATION IS BEING EXPLOITED
BY MULTINATIONAL CORPORATIONS

In Chapter 2, we defined multinational corporations as those companies, such as the Coca-Cola Company, that have their headquarters in one country (their home country), but have substantial operations in many other countries. Many of these multinational corporations generate much or most of their income from operations outside their home country. As you might imagine, they are also very large companies that span the globe. The sales of the biggest companies dwarf the total gross domestic product (GDP) of many countries, as shown in Table 4.4. As the table shows, Wal-Mart Stores was the largest multinational corporation in the world in 2002. Its sales of $246.5 billion totaled more than the GDP of Sweden, Austria, Greece, Ukraine, Malaysia, and Portugal. The next largest companies were General Motors and two oil companies, Exxon and Royal Dutch/Shell, which had sales greater than the GDP of at least 60 countries, including industrialized members of the European Union such as Denmark and Finland.

Most MNCs, like Coca-Cola and General Motors, began their commercial history as domestic companies and then expanded abroad for a number of reasons. Some searched for additional markets, others for raw materials, while still others shifted production to take advantage of lower wages in order to keep costs down. In the late 1950s and early 1960s, many American corporations had little choice but to shift some of their manufacturing to the Western European countries that had formed the European Economic Community. This was because goods exported from the United States to these countries were subject to high tariffs, which local companies did not have to pay. American companies that produced products in EEC countries were treated as domestic companies and therefore could better compete with other local manufacturers. Whatever the reason for expanding beyond their home country, MNCs have been accused of abusing their size by exploiting the globalization process. For example, some MNC activities that have been criticized include transferring technology out of their home country, exploiting workers in developing countries, exporting jobs abroad, and depriving nations of their sovereignty. Let us examine each of these claims in detail.

The Transfer of Technology Argument

Since the 19th-century Industrial Revolution, nations have attempted to preserve whatever technological advantage they had. The British, for example, did not permit the export of technology developed during the Industrial Revolution. However, preventing the transfer of technology proved to be a difficult task, as exemplified by the case of the power loom. Successful power looms were operated in England by the early 1800s, but those made in America were inadequate. British law prevented the exportation of blueprints of patented inventions to other countries. An American entrepreneur named Francis Cabot Lowell realized that for the United States to develop a practical power loom, it would have to utilize British technology. Thus, while visiting English textile mills, Lowell memorized the workings of their power looms. Upon his return, he recruited master mechanic Paul Moody to help him recreate what he had seen. They succeeded in adapting the British design, and the machine shops established by Lowell and Moody at mills in Waltham, Massachusetts, continued to make improvements in the loom. With the introduction of a dependable power loom, the American textile industry was underway.

Today most industrialized nations respect each other's patent laws, which tend to reduce the smuggling or use of someone else's technology. MNCs, however, have been accused of exporting technological expertise from their home countries.[21] Some believe that even in those cases where an American MNC licenses the production of its product abroad, it gives away technology developed by Americans who were educated at public expense.

Of course, this is an oversimplification, in that not all American college and university students are educated at public expense, and many MNCs manufacture or provide products that contain "soft" or "low" technology. Cosmetic, soap, detergent, cereal, and textile manufacturers, for example, transfer little technology of any consequence.

That still leaves companies like IBM, Intel, Cisco, Microsoft, and other high-technology producers. Don't these companies take their technology to wherever they are located? The answer is that these high-tech companies usually do not license or transfer their technology to anyone else. Intel subsidiaries located in India or Israel do not share their technology with any other country or company, other than another Intel subsidiary. All the technology that is developed is owned and marketed by the parent company located in the United States. There have been exceptions to this. For example, in the 1950s, the British company Rank acquired the worldwide rights to Xerox's

How Search for Headache Remedy Spawned Global Industry

- Coca-Cola started life in Atlanta in 1886, the result of a search for a headache remedy.

- It is now the biggest selling and most popular soft drink in history.

- The first international bottling plants opened in 1906 in Canada, Cuba, and Panama.

- Among its brands are Sprite, Dr Pepper, Bacardi Mixers, Nestlé, Nescafé, Schweppes, and Fanta.

- More than 13,000 Coca-Cola beverages are consumed every second of the day, reaching six billion consumers.

- 70 percent of its income comes from outside the United States.

Source: Oliver Duff, July 25, 2003. Copyright © 2003 The Independent. Reprinted with permission.

technology outside of the United States. The transaction netted large profits to Rank at the expense of Xerox. Today, Xerox does not license or transfer its technology to other firms.

On the contrary, many developing countries claim that MNCs do not transfer enough technology to their shores. Some leaders of developing countries complain that the lack of technology transfer is the result of deliberate actions by technology suppliers to maintain monopolies.[22] However, according to Professor Joel Cohen of the University of London, the lack of technology transfer to developing countries is limited mainly by the quality of the education system and the technical skills of the workers; problems with the existing infrastructure, such as transportation, communication, and power systems; characteristics of the production system; and so on. As Cohen notes, "Rigid or ineffective bureaucracies, specific political conditions, high rates of illiteracy, social violence, political instability and frequent labor strikes" work to limit the transfer of technology.[23] Before serious technological transfer can take place, developing countries will have to improve their educational and financial institutions, such as banks and universities, in order improve their ability to absorb it.

DOES GLOBALIZATION HARM WORKERS' INTERESTS?

In 490 B.C., Phidippides, the most celebrated runner in antiquity, arrived in Athens at the end of his final race. He was carrying news of a great Athenian victory in the face of overwhelming odds against Persian forces on the plain of Marathon, 26 miles away. Legend tells that Phidippides arrived in Athens and with his last breath uttered the word "*Nike*"—the name of the Greek goddess of victory—before he collapsed and died. His achievement inspired one of the showpiece events of the modern Olympic Games and, much later, the brand name for the Blue Ribbon Sports Company, now known as Nike.

Sportswear made by Nike and other manufacturers such as Puma, Adidas, Fila, and Reebok were worn and promoted at the 2004 Olympic Games in Athens, Greece. These products are manufactured in developing countries such as China, Cambodia, Thailand, and Turkey by local contractors who are supervised by the MNCs, and the sportswear is imported to countries around the world (Nike, for example, has 900 such contractors). Sportswear is a low-technology product that can be produced with a small capital investment and by semiskilled labor. In order to keep costs down, these products are produced in developing countries. On the surface, there is nothing wrong with this; these companies provide employment for thousands of workers who might not have alternative means to make a living. However, according to some international trade unions and Oxfam (a development, advocacy, and relief agency working to put an end to poverty worldwide), workers in developing countries are being exploited.[24] Examples of the alleged exploitation include 16- to 18- hour workdays, working 7 days a week at rates of pay below the minimum wage set by the host governments, employing child labor, and denying workers the right to form labor unions.

Is there any evidence to refute these charges? Companies like Nike, Adidas, and Puma have established codes of conduct to improve working conditions in the contract factories. Such codes set safety and age standards, legally mandated work hours, and provisions for monitoring the codes. Moreover, Nike and Gap, along with the World Bank and the International Youth Alliance have formed an NGO (non-governmental organization) called the Global Alliance for Workers and Communities, which aims to improve the working lives of people in developing countries and to monitor the factories of global companies' subcontractors. The Global Alliance undertakes surveys of factory workers in developing countries to identify their aspirations. Once these aspirations are determined, education and training programs are created to upgrade the workers.

Another NGO comparable to the Global Alliance is the Fair Labor Association (Figure 4.3), whose mission is also to improve working conditions in developing countries. Members of this organization include Adidas, Eddie Bauer, Gear, Gildan Activewear, Liz Claiborne, New Era, Nordstrom, Nike, Patagonia, Phillips-Van Heusen, Puma, Reebok, and Zephyr. These companies maintain 3,000 factories in 80 countries. By adhering to the Fair Labor Association guidelines, they have committed themselves to self-imposed codes of conduct, to both inside and outside monitoring, and to comply with international labor standards.

Another body that monitors working conditions is the International Labour Organization (ILO) (Figure 4.4). The ILO was created in 1919 primarily for the purpose of adopting international standards to cope with the problem of labor conditions involving "injustice, hardship, and privation." It became the first specialized agency of the UN in 1946. Member nations that have ratified the ILO conventions are monitored for compliance. Complaints also may be brought against non-member counties as well. However, the correction of any deviations from the organization's conventions is voluntary for both members and non-members.

Given the activities of NGOs and labor unions, it is fair to ask whether working conditions have improved in developing countries. The consensus is that they have, but there are still those who are employed under poor working conditions. Much of the blame falls on the governments, rather than on the corporations, for it is governments that determine the work standards and enforce them. True, multinational corporations should adopt standards that do not cause suffering and deprivation. But it is government that must take the initiative to move standards upwards. The Cambodian government recently took a step in that direction when it required manufacturers to be inspected by ILO monitoring teams before receiving export licenses. This ensures that the country's manufacturers will only be able to secure contracts with MNCs by providing evidence that they have decent working conditions.[25]

Figure 4.3 The Fair Trade Association sets out their aims and goals under the "Welcome" banner of the home page of their Website.

The Export of Jobs

Labor unions argue that multinational corporations export jobs from their home countries to those countries in which they establish manufacturing plants. When General Motors and Ford manufacture or assemble cars in Mexico, Great Britain, and France, the argument goes, they are employing workers in those countries at the expense of American workers. An extreme example of locating production abroad is Levi Strauss & Co., which over time has transferred all of its jeans apparel manufacturing

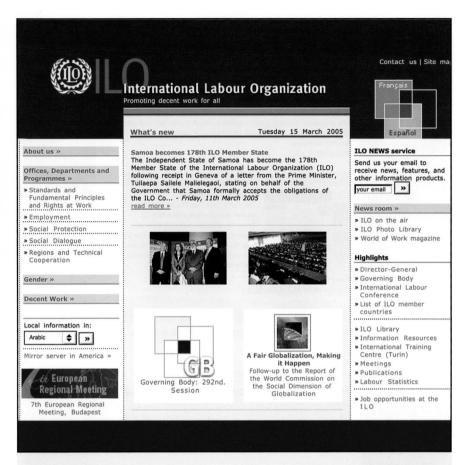

Figure 4.4 The home page of the Website for the International Labour Association states their mission—"Promoting decent work for all." Their site includes information for visitors as well as news to keep their members informed.

out of the United States. Another example is the **outsourcing**, or farming out, of tasks to other firms instead of doing them in-house. Examples include the transfer of call centers, administrative work such as checking credit card references, and data analysis to countries like India. General Electric has some 11,000 Indian employees, mostly agents in call centers and workers who analyze credit card data and market trends. A report by Mitial International[26] estimated that about one-third of Great Britain's call centers will close, resulting in a loss of 90,000 jobs. An

American company, Convergys Corporation, plans to move at least 100 technical support jobs to an overseas center.[27] International Business Machines (IBM) plans to shift up to several thousand skilled software jobs from the United States to India, China, and other countries. According to estimates of International Data Corporation, foreign workers performed about 5 percent of information technology services for American companies in 2003, but that share will increase to 23 percent by the year 2007.[28] Cost reduction is the primary motivation behind outsourcing. The difference in wage costs for skilled workers in developed and developing countries can be substantial. In India,

Levi's Last U.S. Workers Mourn Loss of Good jobs

Clara Flores once thought she had the job of a lifetime, even, perhaps the most solid job in America. She made blue jeans. Not just any blue jeans. Levi's. "It was the original," Flores said. "Wherever you went, it was the same Levi's blue jeans." The . . . company was founded 150 years ago by Levi Strauss, a Bavarian immigrant who settled in San Francisco to outfit gold miners. It has turned out more than 3.5 billion pairs of the sturdy denim jeans with their trademark rivets at the seams and little red pocket tab, becoming an American icon.

. . . by the end of [2003], the last pair of Levi's made in America will roll off the sewing and finishing lines at the factory in San Antonio, another casualty of the shrinking home-grown apparel industry that since 1995 has halved its domestic work force in favor of cheaper foreign labor. It will be a setback too, for San Antonio, home to the Alamo.

Levi Strauss & Co.'s last three Canadian plants will close in March [2003]. . . . That's part of a restructuring that will cut the company's payroll to 9,750 . . . the peak was 37,000 in 1996—and leave none of its jeans production in North America. The work will be contracted to suppliers in 50 countries, from the Caribbean to Latin America and Asia. Competitors, with few exceptions, have shifted their manufacturing to those regions or made jeans there all along.

Source: Ralph Blumenthal, *New York Times*, October 19, 2003. Copyright © 2003 The New York Times Co. Reprinted with permission.

a graduate with a Masters in Business Administration (MBA) degree and three years' work experience earns about $12,000 a year compared to $100,000 a year for a person with the same qualifications in the United States.

Locating work abroad has an additional advantage in that it enables companies to work around the clock. Oracle, a software producer, has two development centers in India that employ some 4,000 people. Programmers there continue projects when their American counterparts leave for the day, and vice-versa. Oracle has globalized its work schedules, enabling it to work 24 hours a day.

Not only do jobs shift from one country to another, but they also shift within countries. Workers have always been able to search for better employment within nations and in the United States jobs have always been "exported" from one state to another. For example, a newspaper reported that the California State Automobile Association planned to ship nearly 500 jobs to call centers in lower-cost states in order to reduce costs. Apparently, the higher cost of doing business in California was the major factor in the company's decision.[29] Therefore, the movement of workers from one location to another in search of better job opportunities is not exclusively a global phenomenon.

This discussion seems to provide ample evidence that the process of globalization harms the interests of workers. However, some argue that many of the jobs being shifted overseas are low-skilled positions that American workers would rather not perform. When the American government began formulating NAFTA, the free-trade treaty between the United States, Canada, and Mexico, there were fears that it would encourage American plants to relocate south of the border and to substitute cheaper Mexican labor for U.S. labor. However, the export of American jobs to Mexico did not occur. On the contrary, the establishment of so-called Maquila plants located in Mexico close to the Mexican–U.S. border, engaged in the assembly of mainly electronic products and transport equipment from components made in the United States, prevented the closure of American manufacturers faced with competition from developing countries. Thus, the jobs of many American workers in the electronics industry were saved because of the shift of the assembly operation to low-cost Mexico. Most of the finished products were re-imported back to the United States, enabling the American companies to compete with imports from Asian companies.

Many American multinational companies have invested abroad to defend overseas markets threatened by trade barriers or increased competition. If U.S. firms were to only produce and operate in the United States, they would lose their markets to foreign firms, usually large enterprises from Europe and Japan, as the Goodyear case demonstrates. The same is true for other multinationals that have invested in the United States, thus contributing to employment and income. As was shown in Table 4.3, foreign MNCs employ about 5 percent of the American work force.

CHALLENGES TO NATIONAL SOVEREIGNTY AND IDENTITY
National sovereignty refers to the right of the state to exercise power. Critics claim that globalization leads to a reduction in the role played by nations in their economic policy-making through international trade arrangements, common currencies, international labor standards, and environmental laws. In

Goodyear Tire Corporation

In almost every overseas Goodyear plant location, the company had no choice but to build a plant to hold the market in face of existing or proposed manufacturers in that country. Exporting from the United States to those markets was not a real alternative. Wage differentials, tariffs, other import restrictions, and transportation costs made it impossible for U.S. manufactured products to compete in those markets . . . In almost every instance, if Goodyear had not established a factory abroad, another manufacturer—very probably foreign—would have.

Source: Goodyear International Corporation.

today's world, nations are becoming increasingly more dependent upon one another. Businesses in one nation trade with businesses in many others. If Japanese manufacturers want to sell home electronic products and appliances in the United States, the products have to meet safety standards and be certified by the Underwriters Laboratory (UL) and operate at 110–120 volts. If American manufacturers want to sell similar products in Europe, they have to comply with standards set by the European Union and individual nations that may be different than those existing in the United States. In these examples, by complying with the standards of other countries, Japanese and Americans lose some of their national sovereignty. In general, the more a nation is integrated into the world economy, the more it is affected by the economic and political events of other countries.

A nation's ability to monitor and supervise the financial dealings of its dependents abroad, including those of home country subsidiaries, is becoming more limited. For example, Fruehauf was an American company that manufactured truck trailers and was headquartered in Indianapolis, Indiana. It had a majority ownership in a plant in France. The French plant entered into a contract with China at a time when the United States had an embargo against sales to China. The U.S. government told Fruehauf that its subsidiary could not sell goods to China. The French government put the subsidiary under the control of France and ordered the subsidiary to go through with the sale. Neither the French nor the U.S. government wished to give up national sovereignty in the determination of whether the sale would be made. The question here is whose laws, regulations, and tax codes apply in a case involving the subsidiary of a multinational corporation—those of the home country or those of the host country?

Countries may elect to give up some of its sovereignty if international trade will benefit its population by increasing employment and income. However, larger countries such as the

United States or Germany may lose less sovereignty than smaller nations, because their domestic market is larger and because their influence in international bodies is greater. For example, a nation that is a member of many international bodies, such as international governmental organizations (IGOs) like the International Labour Organization and the International Monetary Fund, and economic blocs like the European Union or Asian Pacific Economic Community voluntarily gives up some of its sovereignty because it believes that the gains will be greater than the costs. On the other hand, nations that are experiencing economic difficulties, such as high inflation, unemployment, and/or budget deficits will have to surrender some

Fruehauf in France

In 1964 the Treasury Department learned that Fruehauf's French subsidiary had entered into a contract to supply trailers to a French truck manufacturer for assembly and eventual delivery to China. At that time U.S. commercial relations with the People's Republic of China were prohibited by the Trading with the Enemy Act, but were both legal and encouraged in France. The Treasury Department demanded that the American headquarters of Fruehauf force their subsidiary to withdraw from the contract, under penalty of the law.

Several points are of interest here. First, France considered the subsidiary a French firm subject to French law and policy while the American government clearly considered it subject to its law and policy. Second, the U.S. government did not go to the subsidiary directly, but exercised its control over the headquarters located within the borders of the United States and thus exercised its will through the hierarchical structure of the MNE [Multinational Enterprise]. While there is no question that Fruehauf's corporate headquarters is a U.S. firm within U.S. jurisdiction, from a French point of view, the U.S. government implemented its law extraterritorially through the subsidiary of a multinational.

Source: Stephen J. Kobrin, "Sovereignty at Bay: Globalization, Multinational Enterprise, and the International Political System," in Alan Rugman and Thomas Brewer (eds.), *The Oxford Handbook of International Business*. Copyright © 2001 Oxford University Press. Reprinted with permission.

sovereignty to bodies such as the International Monetary Fund or the World Bank in order to receive financial assistance. For example, in the 1990s Mexico experienced a financial crisis and had to apply for financial assistance from the International Monetary Fund. In return, the Mexican government had to relinquish some of its sovereignty over its internal economic affairs and agree to put its "financial house" in order according to requirements imposed by the IMF. One writer compares international trade with marriage.[30] Marriage requires some loss of sovereignty on the part of both bride and groom. Then why do people marry? Because there are perceived benefits relative to the costs. Many couples remain married even when it is evident to others that there are severe deficits in the relationship. The same is true with international trading relationships.

GLOBALIZATION AND FINANCIAL INSTABILITY— THE WORLD FINANCIAL CRISES

For many years Thailand had been praised as one of the so-called Asian Tigers, along with Hong Kong, Indonesia, Malaysia, Singapore, South Korea, Taiwan, and the Philippines, whose economies grew very strongly during the 1980s and 1990s, mainly owing to export industries that had developed with infusions of foreign investment capital. Multinational corporations increased their investment in those countries to take advantage of low wages, and political and economic stability. However, in 1997, a financial crisis erupted in Asia. It started with the collapse of some banks in Thailand and spread to Indonesia (Table 4.5). The Indonesian domestic currency, the rupiah, lost almost 30 percent of its value in one day. The economic loss caused by the Asian financial crisis was estimated to push some 22 million people below the poverty line.[31] The Asian financial crisis is a case study in the way financial crises can arise. The upheaval that started in Thailand shows how a financial shock originating in one country can have enormous repercussions in the rest of the world (Figure 4.5).

Table 4.5   **A Brief Chronology of the Asian Financial Crisis (1985–1998)**

Thailand	From 1985–1995, the economy grew by 9 percent. On May 14–15, the *baht* (local currency) was hit by speculators and lost half its value.
South Korea	The Seoul stock exchange fell 4 percent on November 7, 1997; the next day it dropped 7 percent and on November 27, by 7.2 percent.
Indonesia	At the beginning of 1997, Indonesia had low inflation, a trade surplus (more exports than imports), more than $900 million of foreign exchange and reserves of $20 billion. Influenced by the crisis in Thailand, the *Rupiah* lost its value and stock prices fell.
Malaysia	In 1997, the Kuala Lumpur stock exchange fell by 856 points. In 1998, construction activity fell by 24 percent; manufacturing by 9 percent; and agriculture by 6 percent.

Another financial crisis occurred in Argentina during 1989. Through budget deficits and printing money, the Argentine government touched off a disastrous wave of inflation that led to the virtual disappearance of the currency. Price increases had reached an annual rate of 5,000 percent. Prices were readjusted every day. Moreover, Argentina defaulted on a debt repayment to the World Bank of more than $800 million.

Argentina declared that its currency, the peso, from now on would be worth as much as the U.S. dollar. To prevent the government from resorting to printing more banknotes, it was stipulated that the total currency in circulation in the country would be strictly indexed to the number of dollars held by the central bank. As a result of the crisis, Argentina gave up all monetary autonomy. The linking of the peso to the dollar had the effect of restoring confidence, although it meant that the government relinquished most of its control over its currency. This meant that if the dollar became stronger, the peso would become stronger, but if the dollar weakened, the peso would

Figure 4.5 The finance minister of Thailand, Thanong Bidaya, announced his government's decision to seek a standby credit line from the IMF (International Monetary Fund) on July 28, 1997. At that time Thailand was struggling to stabilize its financial system after it devalued its currency, the *baht*, on July 2, 1997.

likewise weaken. However, knowing that their assets, savings, and investments were convertible into dollars at a preset exchange rate, Argentines and foreigners working in the country began to use the national currency again without fear of losing their assets.

Was globalization the main cause of these financial crises? According to the Indonesian Ambassador at the time, a major cause of the Indonesian crisis was the result of currencies flows out of the country.[32] It is true that as the crisis deepened, investors pulled out whatever capital they could, thus worsening the situation. The crisis also led to an increase in anti-Western sentiment and recriminations against the IMF. However, the crisis was triggered not by foreign investors or multinational corporations, but rather by inherent weaknesses in the economic structures and policies of the countries and the way they were governed. In Indonesia, for example, the economy was controlled to a large extent by then-President Suharto and his family. There was little or no supervision over the banking systems. Globalization helped mitigate the crisis, as Western companies kept their markets open to products produced in Asian countries and agencies such as the International Monetary Fund loaned billions of dollars to help the beleaguered countries.

Consequences of the Crisis

The economies of the United States and Japan were indirectly affected by the crisis in Asia (also dubbed the "Asian flu"). While these large economies did not collapse, the Dow Jones industrial average fell 554 points, or 7.2 percent on October 27, 1997, while the Tokyo Stock Exchange dropped 536 points, or 3 percent, on October 23, 1997. Japan was affected because Asia was its largest market, accounting for 40 percent of its exports. Because of the loss in exports, growth of the Japanese economy slowed from 5 percent to 1.6 percent annually during 1997.

There were also political consequences. President Suharto of Indonesia and the government of Chavalit Yongchaiyudh of Thailand were forced to resign. However, the IMF came to the rescue of both Thailand and Indonesia, the two countries hardest hit by the crisis. A rescue package of $20 billion was approved for Thailand and $23 billion for Indonesia.

At this writing, most of the Asian countries have experienced economic recovery since 1999, and their growth rates have improved considerably. The South Korean, Hong Kong, Taiwan, and Malaysian economies are growing at about 5 percent annually, while Singapore and Thailand have shown growth rates of 3 percent. Almost all of these countries have commenced the restructuring of their financial institutions, although nepotism (the favoring of relatives and friends) in management and government has not been eliminated. Further recovery is dependent on full disclosure of accurate and up-to-date information about the functioning of financial institutions in Asia, so that remedial action can be taken when there are signs of impending problems.

What Does Globalization
Mean to America?

The great rule of conduct for us in regard to foreign nations is, in extending our commercial relations, to have with them [the nations of Europe] as little political connection as possible.
—George Washington's Farewell Address

If George Washington's words, contained in his 1797 Farewell Address to the People of the United States, were followed today, the United States would not have entered into any trade agreements such as NAFTA. Indeed, if he were alive today, America's first president would be considered to be anti-globalization. Has Washington's advice been taken by America's leaders? To what extent has the United States influenced and become influenced by globalization? These are among the issues that will be discussed in this chapter.

GLOBALIZATION AND THE AMERICAN ECONOMY

Most nations can only react to globalization; they are not able to seriously influence it. Only nations that have strong economies and are politically dominant on the world scene, such as the United States,

Japan, Germany, and Great Britain, have been able to affect the direction and speed of the globalization process. Given its sheer size and economic strength, the United States is probably the country least affected by developments in the global economy.

However, the large size of the American market and the purchasing power of American consumers do affect the economies of many other nations. For example, American consumers account for about 20 percent of the world's imports. Many developing countries are dependent upon the American market to buy many of their goods. For example, American consumers purchase about 31 percent of China's office machines and telecom equipment exports, 21 percent of South Korea's transportation equipment exports, and 17 percent of Taiwan's electrical machinery exports.[33] Any downturn in America's economy resulting in the consumption of fewer imported goods will greatly affect the economies of both developed and developing countries. The saying, "when America sneezes, the rest of the world catches cold" certainly rings true. Nevertheless, the United States, like most other countries in the world, participates in the globalization process. American businesses trade with other business concerns around the world, and American multinational enterprises like General Motors, IBM, Motorola, McDonald's, and Wal-Mart have invested in facilities all over the globe. Foreign trade and the operations of American business abroad affect income levels, the standard of living, and employment levels at home. Let us examine to what extent they are impacted by globalization.

THE AMERICAN ECONOMY AND TRADE

How dependent is the American economy for the sale of its manufactured goods and services to other countries? An indication of the importance of trade to a nation's economy is the ratio of exports to the total value of final goods and services produced within a country's borders (the gross domestic product, or GDP). This ratio is a rough indicator of the extent to which a nation's resources are used to produce goods and services that are sold abroad. It also shows the relation of the value of goods and services purchased from other countries to the value of goods and services produced at home. Up until the early 1970s, the export-to-GDP ratio was about 10 percent for the United States compared to 60 to 80 percent for Western European countries. Although the export-to-GDP ratio for the United States stands today at around 22 percent, it is still significantly below that of other developed countries. What this means is that the goods and services produced in the United States are largely consumed at home, rather than in overseas markets. Thus the U.S. economy is not as dependent upon foreign trade as are the economies of other developed countries such as Germany, Great Britain, and Japan.

THE ARGUMENT FOR TRADE LIBERALIZATION

Even though the United States may be less affected by the globalization process than other countries, it supports liberalized trade and investment. This support is driven by the belief that liberalized trade and investment drives economic growth and creates employment. "Liberalized" trade means that countries open their economies to goods, services, and capital from other countries by removing barriers such as trade restrictions, quotas, and taxes on imports, and restrictions on foreign ownership. Trade restrictions are generally imposed to protect local industry from foreign competition. Sometimes, however, they are imposed because of nationalism. An example of the latter was the banning of Coca-Cola in France during the 1940s, a ban that was not lifted until 1953! The official reason for the ban was that Coca-Cola was detrimental to one's health. The real reason was that the drink was a threat to the national drink of France—wine.

One of the main advantages of free trade is increased competition. In free market environments, firms face competition. With free trade, American firms can compete in France with French firms, in the UK with British firms, and so on. Conversely, French and British firms can compete in American markets.

Open markets lead to more competition, thus keeping prices low for consumers. And, lower prices for consumers mean that purchasing power is increased, allowing for the consumption of more goods. When people have more choices, and goods and services are allowed to flow more easily across borders, nations can more quickly specialize in what they do best. That promotes more prosperity abroad, makes goods and services in the United States cheaper, frees the U.S. economy to pursue better opportunities, and raises living standards over the long run.

Free trade also allows the importation of varieties of goods that may not be available locally. For example, almost any American supermarket doubles as an international food bazaar. Alongside potatoes from Idaho and beef from Texas, stores display melons from Mexico, olive oil from Italy, coffee from Colombia, cinnamon from Sri Lanka, wine and cheese from France, and bananas from Costa Rica. The grocery store isn't the only place Americans indulge their taste for foreign-made products. They buy cameras and cars from Japan, shirts from Bangladesh, videocassette recorders from South Korea, paper products from Canada, and fresh flowers from Ecuador. Oil is imported from Kuwait, steel from China, computer programs from India, and semiconductors from Taiwan.

Imagine the American consumer without foreign goods and services. Car buyers couldn't drive off the lot in 8 of the 10 highest-rated vehicles. A bride's finger would no longer sparkle with the best diamonds from Africa. Restaurants couldn't serve real margaritas, because Mexico makes the only genuine tequila. There would be no titanium to forge the high-tech clubs that help golfers hit monster tee shots. There would be no Swiss chocolate or German cutlery.

The United States imports nuts from 67 different countries, including Italy, India, Turkey, and Bolivia. Variety is the spice of life, and much of it would be lost without imports, including cloves from Madagascar, nutmeg from Guatemala, and pepper from India. In millions of everyday decisions, American shoppers show they're quite aware of the value of imports. Take, for example, the sort of products Americans buy from China. The Asian giant has become one of the leading suppliers of toys, leather goods, power tools, shoes, and electronics to the United States. Americans bought $123 billion in products from China in 2002.

If imports only added variety and quality to the marketplace, they would be a boon to consumers. But foreign goods also help keep a lid on prices. They do it in two ways: by being cheaper themselves and by encouraging competitors to lower their prices. From 1997 to 2002, consumer prices in the United States actually fell for a wide range of traded goods primarily made overseas, such as computers, clothing, toys, and photographic supplies. Prices of television sets dropped nearly 10 percent, video equipment dropped 15 percent, and the prices of computers and peripherals declined by more than 25 percent.

WHAT DO AMERICANS THINK ABOUT FREE TRADE?

Despite the arguments in favor of free trade, many Americans believe that imports are bad for economic growth, production, and employment, and are a "burden" that must be borne to help other nations recover their economic health. This belief is held not only by low-income Americans, but also by high-income earners. The University of Maryland's Program on International Policy Attitudes conducts one of the most comprehensive polls on trade issues. In one poll in 2004, researchers found that high-income Americans lost much of their enthusiasm for free trade as they perceive their own jobs threatened by white-collar workers in China, India, and other countries.[34] The survey found that support for free trade fell in most income groups from 1999 to 2004, but dropped most rapidly among high-income respondents, the group that had registered the strongest support for free trade in the past. The poll shows that among Americans making more than $100,000 a year, support for actively promoting more free trade dropped from 57 percent to 28 percent. There were smaller drops, averaging less than 7 percentage points, in income brackets below $70,000, where support for free trade was already weaker. The

Made in China

You don't have to shop at Pier 1 Imports to see "Made in China." A trip to just about any major U.S. retailer—Wal-Mart, Best Buy, Toys "R" Us, Banana Republic—will turn up troves of Chinese imports that we enjoy in everyday life. We get 88 percent of our imported radios from China, 83 percent of our imported toys, 70 percent of leather goods and 67 percent of shoes. In 2002, the United States imported more than $8 billion in sneakers and other shoes from China, $6 billion in toys, and $3 billion in VCRs. It adds up to 11 percent of overall U.S. imports, up from just 0.5 percent in 1980. What would we do without China? Pay more and have less, that's for sure.

Table 5.1   Stocking Up on Chinese Goods

TOP IMPORTS (BILLIONS OF DOLLARS)		TOP IMPORTS (PERCENTAGE OF ALL IMPORTS)	
8.6	Shoes	88	Radios
6.1	Toys	87	Christmas and festive items
5.6	Input-output units	83	Toys
5.1	Data processing machine parts	70	Leather goods
3.2	VCRs	67	Shoes
2.6	Wood furniture	67	Handbags
2.0	Transmission equipment	65	Lamps and lights
1.7	Data storage units	64	Cases for cameras, eyeglasses, etc.
1.6	Christmas items	60	Drills, power tools
1.6	Video games	56	Household plastics
1.6	Telephone sets	54	Sporting goods
1.4	Sweaters and pullovers	53	Ceramic kitchenware

Source: "Stocking up on Chinese Goods" from 2002 Annual Report, Copyright © 2002 by Federal Reserve Bank of Dallas. Reprinted by permission.

same poll found that the share of Americans making more than $100,000 who would like to see free trade slowed down or stopped altogether nearly doubled, from 17 percent to 33 percent.

However, a national poll of Americans conducted by the Roper Center for Public Opinion Research at the University of Connecticut between December 2003 and January 2004 found that 19 percent of respondents agreed that the goal of the United States should be to "actively promote" globalization, while 40 percent agreed that the United States "should simply allow it to continue." Nevertheless, 29 percent believed that the United States should "try to slow it down" (a proportion close to the 33 percent in the University of Maryland poll who would like to see free trade slowed down), while another 9 percent believed that the United States should "try to stop or prevent it." In this poll, those favoring globalization outnumbered those against, although those who expressed the opinion that the United States should actively promote it declined by 9 percent from a similar poll conducted during the end of 1999.

What is the explanation for the decline in support for free trade? There are two possible explanations. First, the survey was undertaken before the American economy started to recover from a lengthy recession. Second, the findings suggest that anxieties about free trade long held by lower-income Americans and blue-collar workers—who have been losing jobs to cheaper labor markets abroad—have spread to high-income workers as well.

The Downside of Globalization

Natasha Humphries, a former tech worker, used to think she was immune from the downside of globalization. No longer.

She lost her $90,000-a-year job at handheld computer maker Palm last summer—along with 40 percent of the company's software integration and testing department—after she helped train Indian workers in Bangalore.

"Free trade isn't free," says Humphries, 30, who used to have a generally favorable opinion about free trade. "The middle class is paying the cost."

Palm confirms that Humphries and several colleagues were let go. Spokeswoman Marlene Somsak says they lost their jobs not to Indian workers but to advanced technology and "largely higher-paid, higher-skilled people" at Palm's California headquarters who can use the new technology.

Source: Peronet Despeignes, "Income Confers No Immunity as Jobs Migrate," *USA Today* (February 23, 2004). Available online at *www.usatoday.com/news/nation/2004-02-*.

In the long run, however, the level of imports has little negative impact on total employment, since the vast majority of Americans work in sectors of the economy that are not affected by significant import competition. The large majority of America's nonfarm workers, about 85 percent, are employed in service industries such as construction, advertising, and government, sectors where import competition is minimal. However, in times of economic recession, when jobs are scarce, any loss of employment from import competition becomes significant. In the short run, the costs of unemployment can be painful and specific, as jobs leave the country. Investment firm Goldman Sachs estimates 300,000 to 500,000 jobs are lost to foreign countries like India and Ireland each year.[35] While that's just a small fraction of the 130 million total U.S. jobs, it comes while the economy is still recovering from its longest hiring slump since 1939. The Bush administration, despite its free-trade leanings, has taken some "protectionist" actions to limit the free flow of imports and protect U.S. jobs, such as imposing tariffs on imported steel and lumber.

AMERICA'S SUPPORT FOR LIBERALIZED TRADE—
THE BEGINNINGS OF A GLOBAL ECONOMY

Since the end of World War II, successive U.S. government administrations have adopted a liberalized trade and investment agenda. The motivation for this policy was not solely economic, but also political. The political aspect began with the desire of the Allied countries to rebuild the war-torn countries of Western Europe after World War II, partly to prevent the spread of Communism. The U.S. felt that establishing a lasting peace could only be accomplished by restoring trade and investment. To this end, a conference was organized under the umbrella of the United Nations towards the end of 1944 at Bretton Woods, New Hampshire, and led by the United States, Great Britain, France, and Canada. The major result of the conference was the establishment of the International Bank for Reconstruction and Development, now known as the World Bank, with headquarters in Washington, D.C. The task of the **World Bank** was to provide capital to countries in order to rebuild their economies, which it is still doing today. The loans were given at reasonable interest rates and for long periods of time.

The **International Monetary Fund (IMF)** was another important institution that was established at the Bretton Woods conference. The purpose of the IMF was to create an international monetary system that would promote foreign trade. Using a fund created by the member nations, the IMF purchases foreign currencies on application from its members so as to discharge international indebtedness and stabilize exchange rates. The IMF had 184 member nations as of 2004.

Bretton Woods was the first major attempt to restore the global economy after the war. But it was not clear sailing. There was some opposition in Congress; the French and Germans were suspect and the Russians seemed to be interested only in securing an outlet for their gold production. For example, examine the following excerpt from an editorial in the *New York Times* published during the conference:

The proposed agreement [the IMF] sets up a huge machinery and ignores all basic principles which must be adopted if such machinery could hope to be successful. American money poured into supporting weak foreign countries will be worse than wasted.

The German government also thought that the impending agreement was too cumbersome, while the French thought that they would gain less from the agreement than smaller European countries. However, agreement was reached and 44 nations became members of the IMF. The French had also tempered their earlier objections as can be seen in a statement made by their chief delegate, Pierre Mendès-France:

> [We] may be proud of having inaugurated a new era in the history of these conferences . . . . Because, as it is impossible in the modern world to circumscribe wars, it will be impossible to avoid the spread of unemployment, economic stagnation, excessive economic fluctuations from one country to another with all their train of miseries and sufferings.

The European Recovery Program

Another major American effort to reduce unemployment, hunger, and homelessness in the 16 European nations after World War II was the establishment of the Marshall Plan, named after the U.S. Secretary of State George Marshall. Marshall wanted to avoid a repetition of what he believed was the United States' too-little, too-late response to Western Europe's economic crisis of 1929 to 1931 and its contribution to the rise of Adolf Hitler. The Marshall Plan was a solo American effort to provide European countries with massive economic assistance in order to rebuild infrastructures, including iron and steel facilities and power plants (Figure 5.1). In addition, the program helped in other ways, through technical assistance to industry; funds for the Ford Motor Company in Great Britain to purchase machine tools for the production of cars, trucks, and tractors for export; investment guarantees to

Figure 5.1 On May 28, 1997, then President Bill Clinton presided over the 50th anniversary of the establishment of the Marshall Plan. The Marshall Plan was the United States' effort to provide European countries with massive economic assistance after the end of World War II.

the Otis Elevator Company to modernize British factories; and funds to enable the French aircraft industry to buy propellers from U.S. manufacturers. The plan began in 1947 and ended in 1952. The program cost the American taxpayers nearly $12 billion, plus some $1.5 billion in loans that were repaid. For comparison's sake, in today's dollar value, the program would cost about $180 billion.

RETREAT FROM GLOBALIZATION?

Some claim that the internationalist position taken by the United States after WWII has changed since the 1970s, when the country experienced increased trade competition.[36] While the United States is still committed to a global trade system free of barriers, it has acted to protect American firms from competing imports. Instead of only championing "free" trade, United States' administrations have also demanded "fair" trade. Unfair trade has been defined as "unjustifiable, unreasonable, or discriminatory" trading practices. What constitutes unjustifiable, unreasonable, and discriminatory policies? Some examples may help. It is common practice in the European Union and the United States to pay subsidies to farmers. Subsidies are considered by economists and the World Trade Organization to be discriminatory because they protect domestic producers. Sometimes these subsidies are paid in order to lower the price of produce so that farmers may be more competitive on world markets. Payments of subsidies to European farmers make it more difficult for American farmers to compete. Even though American farmers receive government subsidies, some European produce is taxed when it reaches the United States. The payment of subsidies by both the United States and European governments is contrary to the idea of free trade, even though some might consider it fair trade. Another example of "fair" trade was the 1980s voluntary export restraint agreement between the United States and Japan that restricted the number of autos that could be exported to the United States. The agreement was hardly voluntary, but was imposed upon Japan in order to protect American auto manufacturers.

United States trade negotiators have generally focused their efforts on removing barriers to trade in goods, but have not made a comparable effort to reduce barriers to trade in professional services, such as doctors, dentists, lawyers, and accountants. The issue of foreign professionals working in the United States is one of trade and not immigration. Restrictions do not prevent foreign professionals from living in the United States, but rather prevent them from providing their services. Apart from the difficulty of acquiring a license to practice in the United States, wage laws could prevent an employer (e.g., a hospital) from hiring foreign professionals for the purpose of saving money.

Pressures for protectionism currently come from three groups: politicians who desire to win votes from steel and textile workers and farmers; workers who are genuinely anxious about losing their jobs; and corporations who fear their ability to compete with emerging nations, especially China. Whether or not these pressures will be resisted is difficult to predict. When facing competition from emerging nations like China, American manufacturers have two options that will enable them to compete: to adopt new technologies or work methods in order to cut costs or to shift their focus to different areas in which they can be more competitive. Adoption of a new manufacturing method by the Allen-Edmonds shoe factory is an example of the first option.[37] Allen-Edmonds is one of the few remaining shoe manufacturers that produce all of its output in the United States (98.5 percent of shoes sold in the United States are made abroad). The new manufacturing methods adopted by Allen-Edmonds should lower costs by 5 percent, which should be sufficient enough to keep its production in the United States. The Allen-Edmonds case shows that innovative business strategy can be an alternative to protectionism. The second option is illustrated by manufacturing American products abroad, such as

Nike footwear, produced in Malaysia, or by Wilson sporting goods, manufactured in Ireland.

WHAT DOES WORLD OPINION THINK OF GLOBALIZATION AND AMERICA?

A poll conducted during the end of 2003 and the beginning of 2004 in 19 countries around the world found that a majority of those questioned did not feel that the world "is going in the right direction" and that the United States is "not having a positive influence in the world."[25] Overall, 37 percent stated that the United States is having a positive influence in the world, versus 55 percent who disagreed. Moreover, there was a significant relationship between those who held negative views about the United States and were generally pessimistic about the direction the world was taking. One could infer from this that many feel the United States has considerable influence over the "state of the world." The origin of those polled who held the most negative views of United States influence were Germany (82 percent of those polled), France (74 percent), Argentina (72 percent), Russia (72 percent), and Turkey (69 percent). The only countries in which a majority of those polled expressed positive views of the United States influence were India (69 percent), Nigeria (52 percent), and South Africa (51 percent). Finally, highly educated and high-income people were more likely to have negative opinions. Consider, however, that the opinions of those polled are affected not only by the economic consequences of globalization, but also by political developments as well.

Alternatives
to Globalization

[The] anti-globalization movement is largely the well intentioned but ill informed being led around by the ill intentioned and well informed (protectionist unions and anarchists).

—*New York Times,* 4/24/2001

Are there alternatives to globalization? We discussed the pros and cons of globalization in Chapter 4. Other chapters have hopefully made evident globalization's effects on the way people live, work, and play around the world. What is more difficult to assess is the magnitude of its effect. We concluded that globalization fosters economic growth, thereby creating more jobs. Through liberalized trade, globalization provides less expensive goods to consumers, thus increasing living standards. On the other hand, globalization has been criticized because developing nations do not share equally in the benefits of economic growth. Moreover, it has been alleged that investors from developed countries use substandard working conditions, pay low wages, employ child labor, and ignore environmental protection laws of developing countries. Who are the critics of globalization? What are their concerns and how real are they?

GLOBALIZATION AND ITS DISCONTENTS[38]

The anti-globalization movement is composed of several dozen diverse non-governmental organizations (NGOs) that have rallied their supporters around the common cause of stopping the globalization process. What do these groups advocate? Some examples should help to understand their concerns. Organizations like Global Exchange[39] and the International Forum on Globalization (IFG)[40] are concerned about environmental, political, and social issues. They believe that the sovereignty of individual nations is reduced by international governmental organizations (IGOs) such as the International Monetary Fund, World Bank, and World Trade Organization. They believe that matters such as trade, investment, and development should be left in the hands of local governments and not international organizations. They advocate either limiting the power of IGOs, or dismantling them altogether (Figure 6.1). They also champion so-called fair trade. For example, the TransFair USA monitors suppliers of mainly agricultural products to make sure that the workers are paid a decent wage and that working conditions are satisfactory. The federation certifies producers of coffee, cocoa, tea, bananas, and other fruit that meet its principles. An example of such certification is given in the accompanying picture (Figure 6.2). Certified products are identified by a "fair trade" label. A list of retailers selling these products can be obtained by clicking on the federation's ad or by entering their website.[41]

Other NGOs identified with the anti-globalization movement support activism against multinational corporations. Many of these are radical groups and some labor unions that reject capitalism as a way of life. Instead, they, like the organization United for a Fair Economy (UFE), envision "communities and nations that do not have dramatic disparities of income, wages, wealth,

Figure 6.1 The critics of globalization claim that the developing nations do not share the benefits of economic growth with other countries. This Indian delegate shouted anti-globalization slogans at the World Social Forum conference in Mumbai, India on January 17, 2004. Some 100,000 activists gathered to oppose globalization, saying that it hurts the world's poor people.

health, safety, respect, and opportunities for recreation and personal growth." [42] These are goals that both globalists and non-globalists would agree with, but the question is how best to achieve them. Some believe that only violent protests will influence decision makers, while others rely more on educational campaigns that appealing to religious and civic organizations as well as the general public.

Groups like Corporate Watch want corporations—particularly multinational companies—to adopt socially responsible policies on labor, the environment, and human rights, and to

Figure 6.2 The impact of the Fair Trade movement can be seen in the "Fair Trade Certified" label on these Millstone brand coffee beans, part of the Procter & Gamble product group. In July 2004, Procter & Gamble announced it would expand sales of its more expensive coffees to benefit impoverished growers as well as the environment.

govern their business activities accordingly. They argue that business standards should be mandated by law. To fulfill these objectives, Corporate Watch undertakes research on the social and environmental impact of large corporations, particularly multinationals. It aims "to expose the mechanisms by which corporations function and the detrimental effects they have on society..."[43] But, who would enact, monitor, and enforce laws that would regulate business standards and behavior, except international organizations that are part of the globalization process that these very groups want to dissolve? Perhaps a better way to achieve such goals would be through existing IGOs such as the United Nations. A significant step in this direction was taken in August 2003 by the UN Sub-Commission on the Promotion and Protection of Human Rights when it approved the "Norms on the Responsibilities of Transnational Corporations and Other Business Enterprises with Regard to Human Rights." The norms specify labor, health, and environmental standards and require businesses not to discriminate on grounds unrelated to the job (such as sex, national origin, or race). However, the UN Norms are not binding on member nations and do not specify what sort of controls and sanctions would be used on companies that do not follow the norms or who would police them. Unless member states adopt the norms into their legal systems, compliance would be on a purely voluntary basis. A number of multinational corporations have indeed adopted the norms, including MTV Europe and the Body Shop International.

Another group of concerned individuals includes environmentalists who are determined to protect scarce natural resources, such as air, water, and plant and animal life. While there are many NGOs active in this area, the most vocal is probably Greenpeace. Less known groups include Businesses and Environmentalists Allied for Recycling (BEAR); BankTrack, a network of civil society organizations tracking the operations of the private financial sector and its effect on people and the environment; Coalition for Environmentally Responsible Economies (CERES), the leading U.S. coalition of environmental, investor, and advocacy groups working together for a sustainable future; the Sierra Club, which is the oldest environmental group in the United States, with 700,000 members;

the International Rivers Network, which links human rights and environmental protection groups; and GEF, the Global Environment Facility an independent financial organization that provides grants to developing countries for projects that benefit the global environment. Since 1991, GEF has provided 4.5 billion in grants from funds donated from some 32 countries.

These are just a few examples of the advocacy groups working on environmental issues. In addition, there are magazines and newsletters such as Earth Talk, which are devoted to environmental education and advocacy.

IS THE ANTI-GLOBALIZATION MOMENTUM PICKING UP OR LOSING STEAM?

The G8 summit meeting on June 8, 2004, in Sea Island, Georgia, took place without the protest demonstrations that had accompanied similar international meetings such as the annual World Economic Forum in Davos, Switzerland, and the WTO meeting in Seattle in 1999 (Figure 6.3). Is this an indication that the anti-globalization movement is losing its initiative? Thomas Friedman of the *New York Times* seems to think so. He cites as an example the national elections held in India in 2004. In those elections, a right-of-center political party lost its majority and was replaced by a left-leaning Congress Party alliance. Was the election a signal that Indians rejected the former government's adherence to a globalization policy? Friedman doesn't think so. Instead, he believes that Indian voters had not said: "Stop the globalization train, we want to get off", but rather, "Slow down the globalization train, and build me a better step-stool, because I want to get on."[44] What Indian voters want are more transparency, accountability, education, and the rule of law. According to the Indian-born journalist, Nayan Chanda, editor of the YaleGlobal online magazine, the election "was about envy, anger and aspirations. It was a classic case of revolutions happening when things are getting better but not fast enough for many people."[45]

Figure 6.3 The G8 summit meeting held on June 8, 2004, in Sea Island, Georgia took place without the protests that had accompanied similar meetings. The summit participants included (from left to right): Irish Prime Minister Bertie Ahern, European Commissioner Romano Prodi, French President Jacques Chirac, British Prime Minister Tony Blair, German Chancellor Gerhard Schroeder, Canadian Prime Minister Paul Martin, Russian President Vladimir Putin, Japanese Prime Minister Junichiro Koizumi, U.S. President George W. Bush, and Italian Prime Minister Silvio Berlusconi.

A WORLD WITHOUT GLOBALIZATION:
WHAT WOULD IT LOOK LIKE?

Let us try and envision a world without globalization. From the point of view of those who are pro-globalization, avoiding it is both practically impossible and potentially disastrous. Those not connected to the global economy will miss out on the next economic and social revolution and will be permanently relegated to either slow growth or no-growth and development. Efforts to avoid participation in the globalization process or being unable to participate will have dire consequences.

Even those who minimize the impact of globalization recognize that the increasing amount of world interconnectedness has, at the very least, transformed the way in which countries

operate. It is impossible, for example, to analyze a modern economy without reference to trade or foreign investment. Labor
may not flow freely from one country to another, but the
globalization of production has had significant effects on
employment and wages in many areas of the world. The
production of General Motors and Volkswagen automobiles
in Mexico, for example, has resulted in the employment and
training of thousands of workers who might not have had
another opportunity to acquire both the skills and the income
required to improve their livelihood. The same is true for workers in many other developing countries.

There is evidence that countries that do not erect barriers to
imports experience higher rates of economic growth than countries that try to limit imports. The 2004 *Economic Report of the
President* of the United States cites a study of the economic
progress of 133 countries between 1950 and 1988.[46] Countries
that had more liberal trade practices experienced annual growth
rates in their economies of about one-half percentage more than
countries without liberalized trade. In the 1990s, removal of
trade barriers increased growth rates by 2.5 percent annually.
Thus, increased globalization of trade leads to economic growth.

Consider the complexity and speed of the interconnectedness of people today. In 1975, the airline industry carried about
200 million passengers; today, because of increased competition
and lower costs, it carries almost 600 million passengers every
year. Until terrorism increased restrictions on global travel, one
could basically travel where and when one wanted to do so.
The speed of travel has increased along with the range of
choices. Do you own a mobile phone? If so, you are one of about
130 million Americans who do. In 1987, only 0.3 percent of
Americans owned mobile phones. Over the last several decades,
there has been a dramatic decline in the cost of international
transportation and communication, which not only has facili-
tated (and been encouraged by) globalization, but also may be
its most important legacy.

The spread of chain stores such as Wal-Mart and do-it-yourself retailers such as Home Depot and Lowe's have enabled consumers in both developed and developing countries to acquire a wide variety of quality products at low prices. Wal-Mart or similar superstores open a branch in a community and within a few years some competitors—usually, small local stores—close. This is what anti-globalization advocates call the "Wal-Mart effect." The opening of branches by American and European chain stores is repeated on a global basis and local merchants suffer.

Global media such as CNN, NBC, CBS, and the BBC have enabled audiences all over the world to have instant news reporting directly into their living rooms. Yet opponents of globalization claim that too much Western culture is spreading to other parts of the world, corrupting local culture. Who is right—those citing the benefits of globalization or its opponents?

Suppose that the globalization process stopped. One of the consequences would be a decline of world trade, resulting in rising unemployment throughout the trading world. The poorest countries of the world would also be affected by a fall in aid and opportunities for trade. As we have seen, there are those who argue that organizations such as the IMF and the World Bank take away from the sovereignty of individual nations. However, a weakening of these and other similar institutions would leave them unequal to the task of settling disputes between nations.

What would the world look like without globalization? The country of Singapore was so poor four decades ago that people didn't think it would survive as a country. But it oriented itself to the world economy and now it has a higher per capita income than Britain, which, by the way, had more than a 200-year head start! Recent U.S. history provides another case study. In two decades, 35 million jobs were created. Even at the beginning of the 1990s, some of the prominent "fair trade" advocates were saying that the United States was going to be a nation of hamburger flippers. Since then, 17.5 million jobs were created, many of them of very high quality. If job creation is a major concern, compare the United States experience with that of Europe, which has been plagued by slow growth over the last decade.

Chrysler Motors Company in the late 1970s had accumulated a huge inventory of cars with poor fuel efficiency at a time of rising fuel prices and as a result faced bankruptcy. Lee Iacocca, the developer of the best-selling Mustang car, had just been fired by the Ford Motor Company as a result of disagreements with Henry Ford II. He was quickly hired to be president of Chrysler on November 2, 1978. Iacocca appealed to the federal government for aid, gambling that it would not allow Chrysler to fail when the national economy was already depressed. Although his request sparked intense debate over the role of government in a market economy, Congress in 1980 agreed to guarantee $1.5 billion in loans if the company could raise another $2 billion on its own. Iacocca responded by finding new sources of credit and by trimming operations, closing plants, and persuading labor unions to accept layoffs and wage cuts. He then shifted the company's emphasis to fuel-efficient models and undertook an aggressive advertising campaign that included personal appearances on television commercials. By 1981, Chrysler showed a small profit, and three years later it announced record profits of more than $2.4 billion.

However, one of the strategies that helped Chrysler to rival its American, Japanese, and European competitors in the 1990s was its participation in the globalization process. Until the late 1990s, Chrysler did not have a significant global presence like the other American car manufacturers, Ford and General Motors, which had been building their international operations for over 60 years. In 1995, Chrysler sold 204,000 vehicles outside of North America, while Ford sold 2.3 million and GM sold 3 million. Both Ford and GM built new plants abroad and consolidated their global engineering resources for cost-effective assaults on emerging markets.

Whereas, in the 1980s, about 85 percent of Chrysler's worldwide sales were made in the United States, today this proportion has fallen to only 36 percent. Part of this global expansion was accomplished through the merger with Daimler in 1998 (the company is now called DaimlerChrysler). DaimlerChrysler is the manufacturer of Mercedes-Benz, the top- selling European luxury car that accounts for about a third of the company's total sales. Moreover, DaimlerChrysler owns about one-third of Mitsubishi, the Japanese car manufacturer. The internationalization of Chrysler through its mergers has enabled the company to remain the third-largest car manufacturing company in the world.

THE BOTTOM LINE

With the development of the Internet, satellite communication, cable television, and cellular technology, the biggest barrier to global trade—distance—has ceased to be a major problem. Communication will become increasingly fast and cheap. All of this will make people all over the globe even more connected. Globalization is certain to continue, and as it does, it will encompass more people. The Swedish author Johan Norberg has argued that because of improved technology, developing countries can more easily take part in trade and improve their standard of living to the level of developed countries in a fraction of the time it once took. Development that took Sweden 80 years to achieve has been accomplished by Taiwan in 25 years.[47] Globalization should be an asset for those countries that want to join it.

In conclusion, the question is not whether to globalize, but rather to what extent to regulate and influence globalization's impact on society. As we have seen, the success of global governance is open to debate. Many IGOs, such as the United Nations, International Monetary Fund, and the World Trade Organization, do attempt to regulate and influence globalization by strengthening the international financial system in order to help the poorest countries integrate into the world economy. While their efforts have shown mixed results, a good part of the blame lies with the developing countries themselves because of policies that they themselves have chosen. While the IGOs are far from perfect, without them, the level of financial and economic instability would be more severe.

In addition to IGOs, there are hundreds of NGOs monitoring globalization. Many of these groups lack the financial and human resources to have more than an informative role, but others, such as Greenpeace and the Sierra Club, have had a significant influence in promoting responsible trade.

Continued monitoring by both IGOs and NGOs should insure that the globalization playing field will become more level, encompassing more people who will benefit from it.

Asia-Pacific Economic Cooperation (APEC)—The premier forum for facilitating economic growth, cooperation, trade, and investment in the Asia-Pacific region. As of 2004, the group consisted of 21 members concentrated in Asia and the Pacific Rim (including Australia, New Zealand, China, Singapore, South Korea, the Philippines and Japan, among others) and the United States, Canada, Mexico, Peru, and Russia. Member countries take individual and collective actions to reduce trade barriers and open their markets.

Euro (€)—The European common currency, adopted by 12 of the 15 members of the European Union.

European Free Trade Association (EFTA)—A free trade association composed of four countries: Iceland, Liechtenstein, Norway, and Switzerland. Founded in 1960 as an economic counterbalance to the more politically driven EEC, the immediate aim of the association was to provide a framework for the liberalization of trade in goods among its members.

European Union (EU)—A common market composed of 25 countries in Western and Eastern Europe and Cyprus. The EU represents the largest association of its kind in the world, with a combined population of 500 million.

Free Trade Area of the Americas (FTAA)—An effort to unite 34 economies of the Americas into a single free trade area. At this writing, negotiations are still taking place towards a final agreement among the parties.

G8—World leaders of eight of the world's largest industrial nations, who meet annually to deal with the major economic and political issues that face their domestic societies and the international community as a whole. The eight member nations are the United States, the UK, France, Italy, Canada, Germany, Japan, and Russia.

General Agreement on Tariffs and Trade (GATT)—An agreement established in 1947 by 24 countries with the aim of reducing existing tariffs (a percentage or absolute tax on the value of imports) and other trade restrictions, and settling trade disputes.

Gross national product (GNP)—The total production of goods and services in an economy.

Globalization—The trend towards a single, integrated, and interdependent world.

International government organizations (IGOs)—International organizations that are organized and governed by governments, such as the World Bank, United Nations, and the International Monetary Fund.

International Labour Organization (ILO)—Founded in 1919 by the League of Nations, it became the first specialized agency of the United Nations in 1946. It seeks to promote and protect social justice and the rights of workers.

International Monetary Fund (IMF)—An international organization with 184 members founded to promote world trade.

Multinational corporations (MNCs)—Companies that have their home (or headquarters) in one country, and operations and investments in other countries.

National sovereignty—The right of the state to exercise power.

National treatment—A concept meaning that a country treats the activities of its partners the same as it treats domestic activities. For example, foreign goods, services, and investments must be treated the same as domestic goods, service, and investments, once they have cleared customs and have become a part of the country's internal market.

North American Free Trade Association (NAFTA)—A free trade agreement between the United States, Canada, and Mexico.

Non-governmental organizations (NGOs)—International organizations that are not organized or governed by governments, such as Greenpeace and World Watch.

Non-tariff barriers—Measures intended to reduce imports by means other than taxation. Examples include limiting the amount of goods imported by quotes, requiring strict product standards that are not in use in other countries, and requiring special packaging that increases the cost of the product imported.

Outsourcing—The subcontracting of an organization's services or functions to an external resource.

Standard of living—Defined as the quality and quantity of goods and services available to people.

Tariff—A percentage or absolute tax on the value of imports.

Trade creation—An effect caused by the extra output produced by member countries generated by the freeing up of trade between them.

Trade diversion—The shift of imports from non-member to member countries.

World Bank—A specialized agency of the UN that provides capital to countries in order to rebuild their economies. The loans are given at reasonable interest rates and for long periods of time.

World Trade Organization (WTO)—The only global international organization that deals with the rules of trade between nations. At its heart are the WTO agreements, negotiated and signed by the bulk of the world's trading nations.

NOTES

1. World Watch Institute, www.globalpolicy.org.

2. Migration Policy Institute, Global Data Center. Available online at http://www.migrationinformation.org/GlobalData.

3. Ibid.

4. Michael Mussa, "Factors Driving Global Economic Integration," presented at a symposium sponsored by the Federal Reserve Bank of Kansas City, August 25, 2000. Available online at http://www.imf.org/external/np/speeches/2000/082500.htm.

5. Volkswagen Corporation.

6. Categorizing NGOs, World Bank Criteria. Available online at http://docs.lib.duke.edu/igo/guides/ngo/define.htm.

7. Michael Mussa, "Factors Driving Global Economic Integration."

8. World Trade Organization.

9. Robert Fogel, *Railroads and American Economic Growth*, Baltimore, MD: The Johns Hopkins University Press, 1964.

10. International Monetary Fund.

11. Ibid.

12. "Measuring Globalization: Who's Up, and Who's Down?" *Foreign Policy*, January/February 2003, pp. 60–72.

13. "Measuring Globalization: Who's Up, and Who's Down?" *Foreign Policy*, January/February 2003, pp. 60–72.

14. Joseph Nye, "Globalization and its Discontents," A Dinner Presentation to the Asia Society Hong Kong Center, July 10, 2001.

15. Jay Mazur, "Labor's New Internationalism," *Journal of Foreign Affairs* (January/February, 2000).

16. United Nations Development Programme, Human Development Report 1999, *Globalization with a Human Face*. New York: Oxford University Press, 1999.

17. *World Economic Outlook*. Washington, D.C.: International Monetary Fund, 2004.

18. International Monetary Fund, *IMF Survey* vol. 26 (July 31, 2000): 245.

19. Joseph Nye, "Globalization and its Discontents."

20. Jeffrey Sachs, "Globalization: A New Map of the World." *The Economist* (June 24, 2000): 99–101.

21. U.S. Congress, *Technology Trade*. Washington, D.C.: Congressional Documents, 1980.

22. Goel Cohen, *Technology Transfer: Strategic Management in Developing Countries*. Thousand Oaks, CA: Sage Publications, 2004.

23. Ibid.

24. Oxfam, The Clean Clothes Campaign, and Global Unions, "Fair Play at the Olympics." Available online at http://www.oxfam.org.uk/what_we_do/issues/trade/playfair_olympics_eng.htm.

25. *The Financial Times*, January 23, 2004, p. 24.

26. Alex Whiting, "British Workers Count The Cost of globalization," *Panos* (September 21, 2003).

27. Michelle Kessler and Stephanie Armour, "Increasing Export of White-Collar Jobs Is Cause for Concern." *USA Today* (August 10, 2003).

28. "Report: IBM to Export Programmer Jobs to Asia." *USA Today* (December 15, 2003).

29. "California Auto Club to Export 500 Jobs to Lower-Cost States." *Sacramento Bee* (April 14, 2004).

30. Brian Easton, "Economic Globalization and Economic Sovereignty," *New Zealand Government and Politics*, ed. R. Miller. New York: Oxford University Press, 2001, pp. 14–24.

31. "A Remedy for Financial Turbulence?" *The Economist* (April 15, 2004).

32. "The Role of International Financial Institutions." Available online at www.globalvision.org/program/globalization/roleof.html.

33. Jeremy Leonard, *How Structural Costs Imposed on U.S. Manufacturers Harm Workers and Threaten Competitiveness*, The Manufacturing Institute of the National Association of Manufacturers, December 2003, p.7.

34. Program on International Policy Attitudes (PIPA), Center on Policy Attitudes and the Center for International Security Studies, University of Maryland, January 2004.

35. *Business Week*, December 8, 2003.

36. Richard Stubbs and Geoffrey Underhill (eds.) *Political Economy and the Changing Global Order*. New York: Oxford University Press, 1998.

37. Aaron Nathans, "Allen-Edmonds Keeps Its Shoes on an American Factory Floor," *New York Times* (May 29, 2004), p. C-1.

38. This heading is taken from a book title by Joseph E. Stiglitz, *Globalization and its Discontents* (New York: W.W. Norton, 2003), who himself is tipping his hat to Sigmund Freud's influential essay *Civilization and Its Discontents* (1930), in which the famous psychoanalyst looked critically at human civilization and culture.

39. www.globalexchange.org.

40. www.ifg.org.

41. Fair Trade Certified. Available online at www.transfairusa.org.

42. United for a Fair Economy, About UFE. Available online at www.faireconomy.org/about/index.html.

43. Corporate Watch Statement of Aims. Available online at www.corporatewatch.org.uk/about.htm.

44. Thomas Friedman, "Think Global, Act Local," *New York Times* (June 6, 2004), Section 4, p. 13.

45. Ibid.

46. Executive Office of the President and the Council of Economic Advisers, *Economic Report of the President*. Washington, D.C.: U.S. Government Printing Office, 2004. Available online at http://www.gpoaccess.gov/eop/index.html.

47. Johan Norberg, *In Defense of Global Capitalism*. Washington, D.C.: Cato Institute, 2003.

BOOKS

Cohen, Goel. *Technology Transfer: Strategic Management in Developing Countries.* Thousand Oaks, CA: Sage Publications, 2004.

Easton, Brian. "Economic Globalization and Economic Sovereignty." In R. Miller (ed.), *New Zealand Government and Politics.* New York: Oxford University Press, 2001.

Escaping the Poverty Trap, The Least Developed Countries Report 2002. New York: United Nations Conference on Trade and Development, 2002.

Fogel, Robert. *Railroads and American Economic Growth.* Baltimore, MD: The Johns Hopkins University Press, 1964.

Friedman, Thomas L. *The Lexus and the Olive Tree: Understanding Globalization.* New York: Farrar, Straus & Giroux, 2000.

Heshmati, Almas. *The Relationship between Income Inequality and Globalization.* Helsinki, Finland: The United Nations University, 2003.

Human Development Report, United Nations Development Programme, 2004.

Leonard, Jeremy. *How Structural Costs Imposed on U.S. Manufacturers Harm Workers and Threaten Competitiveness.* The Manufacturing Institute of the National Association of Manufacturers, 2003.

Norberg, Johan. *In Defense of Global Capitalism.* Washington, D.C.: Cato Institute, 2003.

Nye, Joseph S., Jr., and John D. Donahue (eds.). *Governance in a Globalizing World.* Washington: Brookings Press, 2000.

Stiglitz, Joseph E. *Globalization and its Discontents.* New York: W.W. Norton, 2003.

United Nations Conference on Trade & Development. *World Investment Report,* 2004.

BIBLIOGRAPHY

PUBLICATIONS

Business Week

EFTA Four European Nations, Berne, European Free Trade Association,
   June 2003.

Forbes

Foreign Policy

Fortune

Guardian

Independent

International Chamber of Commerce

The Economist

The New York Times

USA Today

Washington Post

SELECTED WEBSITES

http://www.bbc.co.uk/worldservice/programmes/globalisation/
BBC World Service—Globalization, provides information about multinational
corporations and cultural globalization.

http://www.eurostep.org/detail_page.phtml?page=index
European Solidarity towards Equal Participation of People, an NGO that monitors the
European Union's role in development. The NGO advocates increased civil
participation in trade and development issues.

http://www.theglobalist.com/
The Globalist, a daily online magazine on the global economy, politics, and culture. A
very good site for articles on globalization.

http://www.sociology.emory.edu/globalization/
The Globalization Website, provides information on globalization by subject area.

http://www.ifg.org/
International Forum on Globalization, an alliance of scholars, researchers, activists, and
writers formed to stimulate thinking about the global economy.

BIBLIOGRAPHY

http://www.oneworld.net/
OneWorld.net, provides basic information about globalization.

http://www.project-syndicate.org
Project Syndicate, a source for globalization articles from 170 newspapers in more than 90 countries.

http://www.worldpolicy.org/
World Policy Institute, an online journal containing globalization articles.

http://yaleglobal.yale.edu/
YaleGlobal Online, an online magazine published by the Yale Center for the Study of Globalization.

Bhagwati, Jagdish. *In Defense of Globalization.* New York: Oxford University Press, 2004.

Cavanagh, John, et al,. *Alternatives to Economic Globalization.* San Francisco: Berrett-Koehler Publishers, Inc., 2003.

Chua, Amy. *World on Fire.* New York: Random House, 2003.

Easterly, William. *The Elusive Quest for Growth.* Cambridge, MA: MIT Press, 2001.

Hardt, Michael, and Antonio Negri. *Empire.* Cambridge, MA: Harvard University Press, 2000.

Held, David, and Anthony G. McGrew. *Globalization Transformations Reader: An Introduction to the Globalization Debate.* Malden, MA: Blackwell Publishing Company, 2002.

Klein, Naomi. *Fences and Windows: Dispatches from the Front Lines of the Globalization Debate.* New York: Picador USA, 2002.

Lechner, Frank J., and John Boli. *The Globalization Reader.* Malden, MA: Blackwell Publishing Company, 2004.

INDEX

PICTURE CREDITS

Eugene D. Jaffe, B.S. (Economics), MBA, Ph.D, teaches in the Graduate School of Business Administration at Bar-Ilan University, Israel. He is a former president of the European International Business Academy and is currently teaching in Denmark at the Copenhagen Business School.

James Bacchus, is Chairman of the Global Trade Practice Group of the international law firm Greenburg Traurig, Professional Association. He is also a visiting professor of international law at Vanderbilt University Law School. He served previously as a special assistant to the United States Trade Representative; as a Member of the Congress of the United States, from Florida; and as a Member, for eight years, and Chairman, for two terms, of the Appellate Body of the World Trade Organization. His book, *Trade and Freedom*, was published by Cameron May in London in 2004, and is now in its third edition worldwide.

Ilan Alon, Ph.D, is Associate Professor of International Business at the Crummer Graduate School of Business of Rollins College. He holds a Ph.D in International Business and Economics from Kent State University. He currently teaches courses on Business in the Global Environment and Emerging Markets: China in the business curriculum as well as International Trade and Economics in the economics curriculum.